The Mystery Fancier

Volume 4 Number 4
July/August 1980

THE MYSTERY FANCIER

Volume 4 Number 4
July/August, 1980

TABLE OF CONTENTS

MYSTERIOUSLY SPEAKING 1
Little Old Men With Whom I'm Only Slightly Acquainted,
    by Ellen Nehr 2
The Dilemma of Datchery, by E. F. Bleiler 7
Spy Series Characters in Hardback, Part III,
    by Barry Van Tilburg. 16
IT'S ABOUT CRIME, by Marvin Lachman 18
Leslie Charteris and the Saint: Five Decades of Partnership,
    by Jan Alexandersson and Iwan Hedman. 21
The Great Merlini, by Fred Dueren 28
MYSTERY*FILE: Short Reviews by Steve Lewis. 33
VERDICTS (More Reviews) 44
THE DOCUMENTS IN THE CASE (Letters) 49

The MYSTERY FANcier
(USPS:428-590)
is edited and published bi-monthly by Guy M. Townsend,
840 East Main Street, #5, Blytheville, Arkansas 72315.
Contributions of all descriptions are welcomed.

SUBSCRIPTION RATES: Domestic second class mail, $9.00 per year (6 issues); overseas surface mail, $9.00; overseas airmail, $12.00. Overseas subscribers please pay in international money order, check drawn on U.S. bank, or currency; no checks drawn of foreign banks, please.

Second class postage paid at Blytheville, Arkansas

Copyright 1980 by Guy M. Townsend
All rights reserved for contributors
ISSN:0146-3160

MYSTERIOUSLY SPEAKING...

NEW ADDRESS: 840 E. Main St., #5, Blytheville, AR 72315.

The letters in response to the last two issues have been very disappointing, but I accept a large part of the blame for that. Installments 18 and 19 of the Nero Wolfe Saga took up a full thirty-five pages of text, and it's been a long time since the Saga has engendered any discussion in these pages. This is quite understandable since, as even I admit, all but the most avid fans of Nero Wolfe must have given up on the articles a dozen or so issues back. Well, the Saga is finished now, and I expect the letters to pick up once again. This is an especially good issue with which to turn over a new leaf. Among its attractions are: no Nero Wolfe Saga; long pieces on the Saint, the Great Merlini, and the mysterious Datchery of *Edwin Drood*. There are also further installments of the spies in hardback series and Marv Lachman's column, as well as a sizeable helping from Steve Lewis's Mystery*File. And above it all can be heard the flap, flap, flapping of Ellen Nehr's size twelve tennis shoes as she grants equal time to the male of the species in "Little Old Men, etc."

Beside the paucity of letters--a disgraceful page and a fraction--the Verdicts section is rather short. Aside from a few reviews from Mike Nevins I've completely exhausted my backlog, so get out those pencils and get to work, folks. I need more of everything, pronto.

At last, here's the skinny on Bouchercon XI. It will be held at the National Press Club at 14th and F Streets in downtown Washington, D.C., October 10-12. Registration opens at 5:00 Friday afternoon. Membership fee is $15.00 for the entire weekend, $10.00 for Saturday only, or $5.00 for either Friday only or Sunday only. Send your check to Bouchercon XI, 1299 National Press Building, Washington, D.C. 20045. The Washington Hotel is close to the National Press Club (the hotel is at 15th and Pennsylvania Avenue), and a limited number of rooms will be held until October 1 at the guaranteed price of $50 single, $60 double, plus tax. Call 1/800/424-9540 if you want one. Less plush than the Washington but still clean and relatively close is the Harrington Hotel (at 11th and E Streets). Rates there are $26 single, $36 double, plus tax. The number for the Harrington, also toll-free, is 1/800/424-8532. I'm inclined to think that it would have been a damned sight more convenient to hold the con in a hotel at which we all could stay, but you know they do things funny in Washington....

Guest of honor this year is Gregory Mcdonald, whom you all know. The program itself, I understand from one of my spies, looks to be dry as dust, but, as those of you who have attended earlier Bouchercons will tell you, it's not the program that makes a Bouchercon, it's the people. Hell, I'd go if there were no program whatever. I *am* going, in fact, and I hope to see a whole bunch of you there. I'm easy to spot, remember? I'll be the short, fat fellow with frizzy red hair, a full flowing beard, and a squint in one eye.

LITTLE OLD MEN
WITH WHOM I'M ONLY SLIGHTLY ACQUAINTED
By Ellen Nehr

It would be a monumental error if the contributions to the detective/mystery literature by the Little Old Men who have woven their way through some of its better pages were overlooked. You know some of them, but perhaps a few of their brothers under the skin have escaped your notice. To meet the requirements of this superficial survey the LOM must be over forty, single, living a life either unconnected with or only slightly adjacent to crime, criminals, and their devious doings. (Because of their overwhelming multifariousness, professors have been purposely omitted and will be clumped in a future dissertation of their own.) Medical doctors, novelists, former seamen, ex-actors, and reporters are all eligible for inclusion here. I've added one sheriff since his connection with real crime is problematical outside of these adventures.

We will find that their parents exercised less than prophetic inspiration when naming these boy children. Perhaps there was a rich uncle in the background. Whatever the reasons, here are some of the names inflicted upon them: Moss, St. George, Asey, Leonidas, Webster, Homer, Elisha, and Pierre. Their descriptions are as varied as their names and occupations would lead you to suppose. Our men are paunchy, clean-shaven, bald, have clear eyes with character lines at the corners (never crowsfeet), bearded (but always neatly if somewhat eccentrically trimmed), witty or carefully spoken, clever but not suave. They are tall, lanky, short, somewhat deliberate in movement and speech, amazingly limber for their ages but always firm in their conclusions and convictions.

Geographical spread is another dissimilarity: our characters can be found on Cape Cod, downtown Boston, a swank New York hotel, Virginai, Paris, Colorado, and points in between.

Somewhere in the background there is usually, but not always (fierce independence is another strong point), someone to urge them to finish their breakfast, wear a raincoat, get a haircut, and stay out of trouble. But these people are never romantically or maritally involved with our LOM. A few of these men are determinedly independent, but they are usually the ones who suffer from indegestion. Romance doesn't enter their lives except as a spectator sport, and their contentment at being single is obvious as they flaunt their cozy life-style. After a while you almost begin to agree with that theory, since no one woman could possibly acclimate to their modes of living, and the idea of their ever making any changes is on the edge of preposterous.

"Webster Flagg, erstwhile actor, quandam singer, Negro, was a houseman by day and a man of property by night. Belasco had taught him to serve in the days when playwrights tended to run more heavily toward Negro butlers. Caruso, with whom he had become acquainted while singing in the chorus of Aida, had inducted him into the mysteries of fine Italian cookery. Experience had taught him to save his money." The foregoing is how Virginia Parker Johns discribed Webster in the first of the two books about him. In this one, *Murder by the Day*, we find him working for a variety of people who all have apartments in a building owned by a non-smoking man whose body Webster finds burned to death in a fire-proof apartment. The suspects agree with the police that no crime has been committed, but Webster thinks differently and sets out to prove that murder has indeed been done. In *Servant's Problem* Webster has retired to look after his business and real-estate holdings when he is asked for help by the daughter of an old friend. She is a maid in a brownstone apartment building and has been attacked and severely injured. Webster fills in for her on her job and becomes involved with a man he never gets to see and the man's three nieces who are always around. There are strange things happening in this building, and Webster, in his role as butler, pokes, pries, and eavesdrops until he knows it all. A touch of gang mobsters, a lonesome cowboy, and shady gambling keep the story moving. These are two books where The Butler Did It--solved the case, that is.

There are only three books, so far, about Jim Qwilleran, reporter, ex-alcoholic, and cat custodian. As a beginning-again-at-the-bottom reporter for the *Daily Fluxian* in an un-named mid-western city, he starts out in *The Cat Who Could Read Backwards* by renting an apartment in a house owned by his newspaper's art critic, who has custody of the cat Koko who proves to be of enormous help when his master is murdered. Jim solves the case after a dizzy tour of the art happenings and expositions of the city. In *The Cat Who Ate Danish Modern* Jim and Koko become better acquainted as another murder is discovered and eventually solved. *The Cat Who Turned Off and On* is about Junktown, the part of the city where antiques are sold, displayed, and often parlayed into murder and worse. Jim ends up with an appreciation of some of the finer things in life and a reputation for detecting, and Koko gets a roommate.

Sheriff Moss Magill is the central character in just three books by Dorothy Gardner. As the full-time sheriff and sole law enforcement officer in the town of Notlaw, Colorado, he feels that he is as close to paradise as he will ever come. *Lion in Wait* concerns an ancient, toothless lion, Henry, who is billed as ferocious. He is liberated from his cage at the visiting circus and someone is determined to blame him for some murders which have taken place. Moss investigates the art colony where all of this is happening, finds and returns Henry to his warm, safe cage, and solves the case. *What Crime Is It?* takes Moss from Colorado to New York City, accompanied by a hula-girl clock as a clue to a missing man and a murder which took place in Notlaw. With the assistance of the New York police he brings home the clock and the case. The best in the series is *The Seventh Mourner*, which removes Moss to Scotland, much against his will, where he has escorted the ashes of a wealthy widow who had made him the executor of her will. He meets her less-than-grieving relatives, and this book contains the best illustration of "race memory" I've ever read. Moss is walking down a street when he hears a bagpipe being played for the first time. The atmosphere and characterizations are very well done and the plot is highly memorable.

The three stories which involve St. George Peachy, M.D., are told by Barney Forbes, sometimes Washington D.C. newspaperman and resident of Alexandria, Virginia, who keeps finding bodies. *And When She Was Bad She Was Murdered* starts when Barney, being walked by his dog on a cold and rainy night, finds the body of a woman in an empty and supposedly haunted house. He reports the murder to St. George, the Deputy Medical Examiner, who calls the police. A missing sculptor who had been the girl's boyfriend, an unhappy society marriage, a historical resource library, and a rhyming clue on old parchment to a missing treasure, all combine for a fast and sometimes funny adventure. Dr. Peachy is a retired pathologist who keeps a fully strung skeleton hanging in his library. The conversations are light and the background of Washington politics is inserted painlessly. *Another Mug for the Bier* has Barney, now employed again, covering a Senate hearing and discovering the body of a political gossip columnist on Capitol Hill and moving it to delay discovery and to distract attention from the fact that he had had a fist fight with the victim shortly before he was killed by some sort of esoteric poison. Kickbacks, blackmail, the horsey set, other reporters, and Dr. Peachy's assistance all blend, eventually, into a fast and furious plot when Barney testifies before the coroner's jury. That court scene ties up all the loose ends in a better-than-Perry-Mason style. *The Other Body in Grant's Tomb* refers to a steam room in a turkish bath named after the famous general where Barney discovers the body of a former reporter who has gone there to sober up before he gives Barney the information he needs to prepare and expose, for a national magazine, corruption in the town. We see a good deal of seamy life and religious fervor while the bodies keep coming faster and faster. Dr. Peachy flies out to make sure that Barney's body is not next in line, to perform an illegal autopsy, and to straighten the whole thing out. All three stories are fast, witty, and clever, with even the subordinate characters worthy of novels of their own. Too bad there weren't more since this would have made an excellent TV series.

Leonidas Witherall appears in seven novels by Alice Tilton (Pheobe Atwood Taylor). These books have a curious publishing history, having first appeared in England from 1937 to 1947. Some were printed here during and after that period, but the first, *Beginning With a Bash,* didn't come out as a hardback until thirty-five years after it was written. It was published as a long short story in *Mystery League Magazine* in 1933 under the title "The Mystery in Volume Four." This is all the more curious since the stories are uniquely Bostonian. If you like your characters to stay in one place and behave conventionally, don't bother with this series. When he first appears, Leonidas is a janitor in a used and rare book shop in Boston, having returned from an around-the-world trip to a Depression world where all of his investments are worthless. He had taken an early retirement from the faculty of an exclusive boys' prep school, and his ex-students and their relatives frequently appear in this and subsequent stories. Here he ends up helping the young girl who has just inherited the book shop, a young man who has been accused of theft, a gangster's sister, and her boyfriend. Leonidas, in turn, is helped by a very proper Bostonian matron and her cars. These characters dash around Massachusetts evading the police, finding bodies and books, and having long, explanitory conversations in the most unlikely places. Leonidas discovers at the end that he has inherited a lot of money and property in the town of Dalton (Brookline?) and subsequent books in the series all take place there. Leonidas, who is often called Bill because of his cultivated resemblance to William Shakespeare, starts to build a new and modern house in Dalton and is conscripted to serve on various boards and committees due to the shortage of younger men because of the war. He further inherits Meridith Academy, where he used to teach, and is writing or trying to aviod deadlines for the adventure series of books and radio shows about a spy/adventure character named Hazeltime which has become very popular and is bringing in many dollars. Bodies keep appearing in the most unlikely places, and he is always being suspected and must outwit the police to avoid being arrested. The strength of this series, which should be read in sequence, is the deft way the auxiliary characters compliment the plot and perform as perfect foils for Leonidas's thinking processes. Obviously, Miss Taylor had fun writing these books, and even though the time-frame is dated the ideas are fresh and funny.

Homer Evans is the most absolutely annoying male series character that I've ever read. Although most of his adventures take place in Paris and its environs, some of them are set in the United States (Montana, Hollywood, Las Vegas, and Boston). *The Mysterious Mickey Finn* introduces Homer, a wealthy American expatriate, his much-put-upon girlfriend, Marion, and assorted underworld characters who soon become part of the Evans menage. *Hugger Mugger in the Morgue* is next with more of the same. In *Mahem in B-Flat* a missing Guarnerius violin which has been stolen from a visiting Bostonian virtuoso starts this unlikely clan on trips which involve a boat trip on the Seine, more gang fights, pseudo-civilized conversations, and meals than would normally fill three books. Our hero and part of his entourage mofe to the Montana ranch of his girl friend Marion where, in true wild-west style, we mix a tribe of Indians, Parisian characters, and American know-how to combat a range war. *Black Gardinia, The Black and the Red*, and *Waylaid in Boston* involve Hollywood, a cross-country train trip and Las Vegas, and, of course, Boston. Except for the last three, sequential reading is recommended.

The Asey Mayo stories, all twenty-four of them, almost deserve a chapter by themselves. Asey could only have come from Cape Cod where they have been growing men like him for three hundred years. He is a former sailor, mechanic, cook, and everyone's ideal jack-of-all-trades. When we meet him he is more-or-less retired and trying to live a calm life, but bodies keep appearing all over the landscape and people are always getting him involved in murders, kidnappings, assaults, snowstorms, auctions, and historical pageants.

Among his sometimes unwilling assistants are Bostonian matrons, local residents who are in some way related to him, his cousin and Housekeeper Jenny and her husband Sil, and Dr. Cummings who, as Medical Examiner, is frequently on the scene and always being asked just how long the corpse has been dead. He then goes on for several paragraphs of being speechless as he tells us and the world that it is almost impossible to tell, despite what those fellows in detective books say. If you wonder about life during the Depression and World War II just dip into any of these.

Kathleen Moore Knight could have made a writing career out of Elisha Macomber. There are sixteen books about him, starting in 1935 and going through 1960. This is one series in which it doesn't matter where you start, because Elisha never grows older or changes in any way, except that in some of the books his New England accent is a bit more difficult to decode than in others. Elisha is a born-and-bred Yankee who lives where his family has always lived--in Penberthy Township, Massachusetts, often mistaken for Cape Cod but in reality a part of Martha's Vineyard. In one of the early books he is said to be a Harvard graduate, but that obviously hasn't affected his speech or his logical thinking. He owns and runs a fish market and is a landlord of sorts, and is now and ever has been the senior selectman of the area. Elisha is not above circumventing the law or even inventing his own kind of justice when he feels that his homeland is in danger. Almost every book concerns a native returning to the island, or a stranger from the outside world effecting a resident, most of whom Elisha has known from babyhood--either his babyhood or theirs. In two of the books Mrs. Knight has moved Elisha to Panama, where he quickly adapts to local customs and, with his talent for finding bodies, becomes acquainted with the police procedures and officers rather more rapidly than a regular tourist. Ideal nostalgic summer reading.

Pierre Chambrun runs the Beaumont Hotel in New York City in the dozen-plus adventures of his recorded by Hugh Pentecost. Chambrun is a Frenchman by birth and a European trained hotelman, and we are frequently reminded of his youthful days in the French Resistance during World War II. Remnants of his past life frequently surface as he finds bodies, gets kidnapped, has the hotel subjected to bomb and fire threats and the appearance and disappearance of movie stars, past and present. His art-covered office, where pots of Turkish coffee seem to be constantly brewing, is the scene of more confrontations and conferences than Allied Headquarters saw before D-Day. His second pair of eyes and legs is Mark Haskell, public relations man and narrator of these tales, who keeps an eye on the running battle between the guests and the police. Calm and decorum seem to be the ultimate but unreachable goals of Pierre Chambrun, but if you've read one of these you've read them all. Only the names have been changed to protect the copyright.

THE DILEMMA OF DATCHERY
By E. F. Bleiler

[*EDITOR'S NOTE: Although Ev included a prefatory note to go with this article, I think a portion of his cover letter says it better and I have taken the liberty of making the substitution without consulting him. Here it is:*
      I think that in subject matter this is a fairly important paper. It was the first solid attempt to identify Datchery rigorously, and so far as I know there is no reason to alter it. It has been in my file cabinet for many years, and every now and then I have planned to take it out and rewrite it, but have never gotten to it. But as I see from Robert Fleissner's article in the Winter 1980 TAD, the world is starting to catch up with me.
      On its non-publication history. In a splurge of energy in 1954 and 5, I wrote a batch of Sherlockian material and this paper, along with my first version of *Before Poe: The Prehistory of the Detective Story*, and did nothing with most of it. The Sherlockian material got lost by a clown on the West Coast, who planned to publish it then disappeared. And *Before Poe* I decided needed more work and put aside. "The Dilemma of Datchery," if my memory serves me correctly, was never submitted anywhere. I meant to send it to *The Dickensian* but never got around to it.
      So, if you want to publish it, here it is. It will have to be as is, for I don't have the time or inclination to rewrite, and while I might write it better today, I think that it is certainly passable editorially.]

Some eighty-five years ago [1870] Charles Dickens began his last novel, *The Mystery of Edwin Drood*, which was to have been a mystery story in the manner of Wilkie Collins. Like most other devisers of suspense and detection, Dickens undoubtedly intended temporarily to puzzle his readers, and in a backhanded way he was all to successful, more successful, in fact, than any other mystery story writer in any time or tongue; for he died suddenly, leaving *Edwin Drood* approximately half finished, with no clarification of the many minor mysteries which interweave to form the complex plot. But Dickens's death was no barrier to his admirers. Some dozen assorted writers have tried their hands at finishing *Edwin Drood*, building from Dickens's hints and their own imaginations; while scores have written more or less scholarly articles attempting to solve the problems in *Edwin Drood*. Dickens, however, builded well, for despite these articles fanciful and grave, there is still no agreement among scholars as to Dickens's intentions, and *The Mystery of Edwin Drood* is still a mystery.

The plot of *Edwin Drood*, as far as it was written out, is characteristically Victorian in motives and surface treatment. There was, once, visiting in Cloisterham (Rochester, Kent), a young man named Edwin Drood, an orphan, who suddenly disappeared as mysteriously as a magician's assistant. Suspicion immediately fell upon Neville Landless, a young fire-eater whom Drood had insulted and quarrelled with, but no corpse was to be found, and charges could not be pressed. The reader, however, knows more: that John Jasper, marvellous musician, opiumist, guardian and nearly coetaneous uncle of the missing Drood, was madly in love with Drood's fiancée (Rosa Bud), and, amid opium dreams of grandeur and crime, has plotted to murder Drood. Just as Neville Landless is the burn of heat, John Jasper is the shadow of cold. And as the first part of the text closes, we are left with a single major mystery: "What has happened to Edwin Drood?"

The second half of our text, beginning with the seventeenth chapter, is set approximately six months later, and develops the second major mystery: "Who is Dick Datchery?" While John Jasper broods in Cloisterham, "carving devils from his heart," counteraction is emerging in London. There, a circle is gradually solidifying from those whom Jasper has injured. Rosa, Drood's fiancée, has fled to London to escape Jasper's suit; and Neville Landless and his sister have joined forces with her. Hiram Grewgious, Rosa's guardian, is openly suspicious of Jasper. And in Cloisterham, a new personality enters the story: Dick Datchery, a most engaging retired "buffer" with long white locks and black brows, who sits sentinel upon Jasper's movements. And, as our text abruptly ends, a pattern is beginning to shake itself free from the hitherto seemingly random associations and humors. A net is being laced around John Jasper. The Londoners, in varying degrees, suspect him; Datchery has a witness to Jasper's opium ravings. And the net is beginning to close... But the fisherman died and the net was neither closed nor released. Instead, a host of minor fish have been swimming about since June 8, 1870.

Out text of *Edwin Drood* is only half finished, and there is disconcertingly little secondary material to show the trend which the unwritten remainder would have taken, for Dickens wrote no general outline. Indeed, secretiveness and sensitivity pervaded this last novel, and Dickens so resented questions about it that he would give only the most grudging and guarded answers. Even his immediate family and his confidant, John Forster, knew only the barest outlines of the plot, so little, in fact, that all they preserved could be pressed into a single short paragraph which leaves untouched all too great an area. And subsidiary material, like correspondence, and chapter notes, and possible instructions to the illustrating artists are no more than chameleon skins which change color as they are adapted to each successive interpretation of *Drood*.

Our first mystery, nevertheless, the fate of Edwin Drood, is easily disposed of. John Forster is very explicit that Drood was really murdered, and that the London circle will unmask Jasper as the murderer. And our other two sources, Charles Dickens, Junior, and Sir Luke Fildes, who illustrated the periodical numbers of *Drood*, unhesitatingly confirm Forster: Charles Dickens stated clearly in conversation that Drood was really dead. And there is thus no reanimating his carcass, as some would, with printer's ink.

This death is unshakable. But our second mystery, the identity of Dick Datchery, is far less firm, for none of our sources identified Datchery, and those who plan to reconstruct *Edwin Drood* have too many difficult clues to evaluate. That Datchery came to Cloisterham to investigate John Jasper is obvious from the text, and that there is at least a mystery about him is equally certain. No other character is described with such ingenious ambiguity as to at once suggest and undermine the possibility of imposture. From his appearance he is a disharmony. He is at first white-haired with black brows, yet later gray-haired. He has a military air, yet disclaims army or navy. He obviously has a purpose in Cloisterham, yet he pretends to be a retired "buffer" looking for a comfortable haven. And he pays excessive heed to his long hair, continually shaking it, while there are hints (though no more than hints) that he wears a wig. The masterful caution with which Datchery is hedged with mystery truly refutes those who see *Drood* as a total failing of Dicken's powers, for everywhere the author very surely treads a razor-sharp bridge of suggesting infinities and yielding, really, absolutely nothing.

In the critical literature Datchery has been overwhelmingly identified as some other personality in *Edwin Drood* in disguise. The favorites have been Drood himself (who, according to some theorists, escaped Jasper), Helena Landless, Tartar (an ex-naval officer who joins the London circle), Hiram Grewgious (Rosa Bud's guardian), and Bazzard (Grewgious's law clerk). These identifications, indeed, have gone in cycles. The Victorians preferred Drood or Helena Landless; our own age, which sees transvestism differently, has favored Bazzard or Grewgious. Bazzard, all in all, is at present, as Vincent Starrett has put it, "the people's choice," though the most detailed Drood study in recent years, Richard M. Baker's *The Drood Murder Case*, favors Hiram Grewgious.

These varied identifications, unfortunately, have all too frequently been sentimentally conceived, and have been based more upon the researcher's whim than the author's text, for the text, incomplete though it is, presents clear and irrefutable means for eliminating most of the masks which have been advanced, if, of course, we assume that Charles Dickens knew what he was doing.

In *Edwin Drood* there are approximately thirty persons who have both names and speaking parts, and to them may be applied several circles of exclusion drawn from Dickens's complete unedited text, circles which rely as little as possible upon subjective factors. First, several persons are ruled out as true identities for Datchery by their co-presence with Dick Datchery. These are: John Jasper, the Topes, Sapsea, Crisparkle, the Opium Hag, Durdles, and Deputy. (Fortunately, no one, to our knowledge, has yet suggested that Datchery is simply an embodied dissociated conscience for John Jasper.)

Almost all remaining persons, secondly, are eliminated by a single action on Mr. Datchery's part, an action whose astonishing importance has apparently escaped all researchers:

> So when he had done his dinner, he was duly directed to the spot, and sallied out for it. But the Crozier being a hotel of the most retiring disposition, and the waiter's directions being fatally precise, he soon became bewildered, and went boggling about and about the Cathedral Tower, wherever he

> he could catch a glimpse of it, with a general impression on
> his mind that Mrs. Tope's was somewhere very near it, and that
> like the children in the game of hot boiled beans and very
> good butter, he was warm in his search when he saw the Tower,
> and cold when he didn't see it. He was getting very cold in-
> deed when he came upon a fragment of burial-ground.... [*The
> Mystery of Edwin Drood,* Chapter XVIII.]

In this text, which Dickens later trimmed, Datchery is by authorial omniscience officially, unmistakably, and immutably declared, "Lost!" And so, Datchery was a stranger to Cloisterham.

We can now drop, without question, Drood, Rosa Bud, Helena and Neville Landless, Grewgious, and all the establishment at the Nuns' House, for the area of action in Cloisterham is limited; the buildings where the chief characters live are all visible or nearly visible from the Tope establishment. Drood, obviously, knew where the Tope Hotel was--within touching distance of Jasper's Gatehouse, where he had stayed so long; and unless Drood were stricken with amnesia, an explanation hitherto spared us, could hardly become lost in his own frontyard. Neville Landless lived approximately three months, and his sister Helena approximately nine months, within a stone's throw of the Tope hotel, with Helena even being able to see the near vicinity of the hotel. Rosa bud seems to have spent years in Cloisterham. And as for Hiram Grewgious--in many ways the best mask for Datchery--not only is he perfectly familiar with the cathedral area from many visits to the town, but he is even stated to have summoned Mr. and Mrs. Tope when Jasper fainted.

Four persons remain to us: Billickin, Honeythunder, Tartar, and Bazzard. Billickin may be discarded immediately, for this elderly lady who operates a London rooming house can hardly be Datchery, while Honeythunder, who visited Cloisterham once, is an obvious "humour": he sincerely believes Landless to be guilty of murder. We are left with Tartar and Bazzard.

Two more exemptions can rid us of ex-lieutenant Tartar. First, as Mr. Baker has pointed out, Datchery is not entirely sure of the meaning of a slang naval term ("jacks"), which an ex-naval officer, like Tartar, would not have questioned. Secondly, Dick Datchery, in Chapter XXIII, gives us one undisguisable flash of his true identity. When he drops a coin before the Opium Hag, he "reddens with the exertion" of picking it up. And so Tartar leaves us, for much stress has been placed upon Tartar's athletic prowess and almost simian agility, as he clambers over roofs as lightly as up rigging, and hangs out windows like an impossibly reckless glazier. No, Tartar cannot be Datchery, and Bazzard alone of the named characters--or a new personage--remains to us, for Bazzard, though relatively young, has been characterized as sluggish in physique. Bazzard may well redden when he stoops.

Bazzard alone can survive our negative tests; and he can also be reinforced as a claimant by positive evidence. At the time that Datchery appears in Cloisterham--We reject, as utterly without reason, Professor Henry Jackson's conjecture that the chapters in *Edwin Drood* should be rearranged--Bazzard is not in his accustomed place in Grewgious's office. He is--as Mr. Grewgious puts it--"off duty here, altogether, just at present." And, again, Bazzard, whom Grewgious rates highly, is the logical confidant to Grewgious's suspicions of John Jasper. Bazzard is probably a stranger to Cloisterham, though our text is silent here, and Bazzard might well have to wear a disguise, for it is very likely that Jasper has seen him. Bazzard, too, is enamoured of the stage. He wrote a play called "The Thorn of Anxiety", and may be familiar with make-up and board-strutting. All this evidence, negative and positive, brings us to the conclusion that Dickens intended that the reader identify Datchery and Bazzard. Please note, however, that this is not the same as saying that Datchery *was* Bazzard.

A peculiarity of *Edwin Drood* must now be mentioned, a highly significant peculiarity: that it is damnably hard to prove one's own theory, but relatively easy to cloud one's opponent's theories. And Bazzard, despite his success in running the negative gauntlet, is very vulnerable. The attack moves in two lines: against Bazzard the actor, and against Bazzard the man. First, point out the opponents of Bazzard, too much has been read into "The Thorn of Anxiety." Dickens is very explicit in saying that Bazzard wrote a play, and that he is a member of a coterie who dedicated their (presumably bad) works to one another. Dickens is here obviously satirical. There is absolutely no hint that Bazzard ever acted, or even understood the art of makeup. A dramaturge is not the same as an actor. And Datchery, if merely an assumption by a named character, is the summit of incredibly able acting.

Argument two: Bazzard, as described, is simply too weak to bear the weight of Datchery. Bazzard, as he appears in Chapter XI, is a surly, self-pitying egotist, ostentatious in mock-humility; a glutton, and a boor. He is only a humour, a sort of reverse Uriah Heep. Can such a person, argue his opponents, be the witty, mellow, logical, sensitive Datchery, whose devious and nimble mind can ensnare a half-dozen asses and apes in their own stupidity; whose vagrant fantasy can see the workings of fate in an ancient inn-reckoning? No more, say the anti-Bazzardites, than Pistol could have impersonated Hamlet.

§   §   §

We have worked ourselves into a mild dilemma: our leading suspect for Datchery-ship stands insecure in essence. What shall we do? We shall now recognize that Bazzard's postscriptal antics are not isolated, but part of a pattern, for *Edwin Drood* is nothing more than an enormous quagmire of false trails and quicksands. Hardly a direction is put forth without, in near sequence, its cancellation and then--its reemergence. These trails--as is the case with Bazzard--lead in all directions, but arrive nowhere. And it is these false trails, we feel, that have misled previous researchers, most of whom have cantered along a single one--and defended it--rather than examining the web of roads.

The name of this web is "deliberate misdirection." Let us consider only two plot questions, although many more could be similarly anatomized. Is Drood dead? Pro: John Jasper has as good as confessed guilt; once, in words, to Rosa Bud; another time, in action, to Grewgious. Con: no corpse has been found, and (we must emphasize) Jasper, in strict logicality, had no reason on earth to conceal the body if there was one. His plans included "framing" Neville Landless, and had there been a corpse available at the proper moment, Landless would have hanged. Pro: the book abounds with symbols and overtones of death. Con: survival hints are also present. A chapter heading, "When shall these three meetagain," and the cover illustration which was drawn to Dickens's specifications, can be interpreted, if ingenuity be exercised, as indicating that Drood survived.

The same conflicting evidence can be found in the question of Datchery's true identity. It is not simply perverseness, or inability to read plain English, or madness which has boxed the compass to find the man, or woman, of whom Datchery is a facet. It is Charles Dickens himself, who has carefully scattered dozens of hints, misleading and genuine, for his readers. Is Datchery a new character, and not simply a mask for another personality? Pro: he is different in appearance and personality from all other characters. Con: consider his disingenuous actions, the matter of his possible wig. What is his identity, if a mask? Perhaps Helena Landless: she has motive, intellect, and is apt in theatrical makeup. She delighted, when younger, in male impersonation. Grewgious? He is the first, apparently, to suspect Jasper's guilt; he has announced his intention to have Jasper watched; he is preoccupied with his hair, as is Datchery; and, most important of all, he is the closest in personality, mental powers, and (inferred) age to Dick Datchery. The scale is truly heavily swung for Grewgious (though, of course, he is really eliminated). Bazzard? Weighted down, as we have seen with clues.

All these clues and suggestions are mutually contradictory, but they form, nevertheless, a pattern. And that pattern is deliberate misdirection. Charles Dickens very obviously tried--with considerable success--to mislead his readers as far as he was honestly able. Ambiguity is the motif of the day.

Bazzard alone remains to us, after the text has been examined, as a possible prime for Datchery. And of Bazzard we are both suspicious and incredulous, for although textual specificities will not demand his destruction, the nuances and overtones of both the story and Dickens's literary personality show Bazzard as simply the greatest and reddest of all red herring, the one that nearly got away with it.

Bazzard, as has often been pointed out, is really unable to bear the weight of Datchery's character, and any attempted reconciliation between his grubby egotism and Datchery's slightly doddering whimsicality, while not impossible, is rendered suspect by Bazzard's own name. It was the practice of Dickens, in *Edwin Drood* as in most of his other work, to name his minor characters with slightly distorted words suggestive of their humour. Here, in *Drood*, for example, Sapsea is "sapsy," a schoolboy's endearing diminutive for a sap; Tartar is a tar; Rosa Bud is, figuratively, a rose-bud; Landless is landless and homeless; Billickin, who dignifies a rooming house, is a billikin, a small domestic utensil; and Bazzard is--a buzzard. (English pronunciation, where the first "a" would approximate the sound of "a" in Bostonian "calf," makes this identity must more obvious than the usual

American pronunciation of "a" as in "cat.") What better symbol could be found for this law-clerk than this filthy fowl?

This name, I am inclined to believe, is a sure indication that Bazzard is only what he seems to be, and a token for believing that Datchery shall not bloom out of Bazzard like a lotus out of mud.

We find a further thread to follow--though, to be sure, a nearly colorless thread--in the circumstances of Datchery's first interview with John Jasper. Datchery, it will be remembered, finally found the Tope establishment, and bespoke lodgings there, dependent, however, upon Mr. John Jasper's giving a favorable "character" to the Topes. Datchery thereupon interviewed Jasper, and learned that the Topes were dependable. This all, at first glance, seems open and undevious, but closer examination of the circumstances shadows out invisible patternings. Datchery, actually, had no reason to seek a reference from Jasper or anyone else. Datchery came to Cloisterham, as all authorities (and Charles Dickens) agree, to watch John Jasper, and the Tope hotel was ideal for his purposes, seemingly the only hotel there. It seems obvious that Datchery, for one reason or another, wished to meet Jasper, and used Tope simply as an excuse to force an interview. Why? For social ends, as we might think in another context? No, for Datchery did not follow up his introduction to Jasper, but, indeed, made no pretense, later, of hiding his dislike for Jasper. But perhaps Datchery did not know Jasper, and simply wanted to identify him?

If we interpret this scene as the trick of a "detective" who wants to learn Jasper's appearance--and we freely admit that this is interpretation rather than authorial statement--Bazzard eliminates himself as an identity for Datchery. If Bazzard knew Jasper, from a possible visit of Jasper's to Mr. Grewgious's establishment in London, Bazzard had no reason to press for an interview. If Bazzard did not know Jasper, and vice versa, there was no urgent reason for a cumbrous imposture and disguise.

Datchery, as a third point against Bazzard, is, to me, obviously an elderly man, not simply a young man in white locks and greasepaint wrinkles. It is age that causes him to redden when he stoops. And he is characterized as an elderly man. He is mellow, socially adept, errantly whimsical, and highly individuated. And for Dickens, as a rule, such individuation as Datchery's, such development of full personality, come only in later life. Young men, for him, are usually uncrystallized, often not far from being only types. Such is the case with all the very young personalities in *Edwin Drood*. Edwin, himself, we must point out to those who dislike him, is not really "antipatico," he is simply calfish and undeveloped. Had he lived, it is hinted, he would have grown. Jasper, Crisparkle and Tartar, as the next level of age, assume greater independence from their biological and environmental moulds, while Grewgious, the oldest named character (save the nearly senile Mrs. Crisparkle), is by far the most complex unquestioned personality in the novel. And this same pattern, be it conscious or unconscious on the part of the author, is to be found in Dickens's other work. Can one imagine a child Micawber? A child Fagin, or Brownlow, or Gabriel Vardan? Or an elderly Oliver Twist or Copperfield? For Dickens true individuation, especially the gift of whimsy, comes in later life, and by all counts, therefore, Datchery is an elderly man. And thereby, he is, of necessity, a new character in *The Mystery of Edwin Drood*.

If Datchery is a new character, two possible identities are most obvious. Datchery may simply be a detective, perhaps hired by Grewgious; perhaps otherwise acquainted with the case. Or, secondly, Mr. Datchery may be a "ghost," a "watcher from the dead"--an exemplar of a theme which seems to have fascinated Dickens.

In much Victorian literature there are peculiar assumptions about the universe. Most obvious of these is the heightening of social intercourse, so that persons known to us keep bobbing up and reemerging in the most unexpected places and situations, a practice which to us moderns is "coincidental" and disturbing. Lives, for the Victorians, intersect like the paths of inked balls rolling about the hollow interior of a paper-lined sphere. (In *Edwin Drood*, for example, Tartar, who enters the story by the bare chance of living next door to Landless, is not suffered to remain a stranger, but is unexpectedly--and incredibly--revealed to be a childhood friend of Crisparkle's.) And besides this, another slightly contradictory permission is yielded: that there is a dim penumbra surrounding each novel, a limbo of biologically necessary persons, who may suddenly precipitate themselves into the story like actors-from-the-wings as long-lost brothers, or uncles, or fathers, or mothers; persons who have been pocketed in time by shipwreck, or loss of memory, or degradation, or captivity among savages, or fortune-grubbing in the New World. One such phantom may be materializing as Datchery.

Or is this, too, one of the misdirections which Dickens calculated for his audience? Note the idiosyncratic vagueness of the text. Rosa's parents are unquestionably dead, but Drood's father is glossed over silently. We know absolutely nothing about him, nor of the peculiar circumstances which gave Drood a nearly coetaneous "uncle." Nor do we know anything of Landless, Sr. The Orient pervades this novel, just as do opium fumes, and either man may perhaps have been resident upon some tropical island, in mild dalliance, until the proper moment.

The father of Edwin Drood could pass all our exclusions and interpretations. He might, upon returning to England unexpectedly, contact his old friend Grewgious, and from him learn of the peculiar situation at Cloisterham. His knowledge of the crime would be second-hand, as Datchery's seems to be. He would be a stranger to the dusty cathedral town, ignorant of Jasper's face, elderly, and he would simply be telling the truth when he refers to himself as a "buffer" looking for a rest--after he has avenged his son.

Datchery brings to his quest not the calm, dispassionate investigation of a professional, but the emotions of a man who feels the crime deeply. He is concerned. His actions and words are those of a man who really hates John Jasper, of a man who takes little care to hide his hatred. Such emotion could well be expected of Drood Sr. (or, less likely, of a Landless uncle) upon learning that his son or nephew has been murdered (or "framed") by a lustful, conniving scoundrel. And his personality, admittedly new to the story, can be legitimately unique; we need invoke no strange transformations beneath the crumbling death of Cloisterham.

1980 Addendum: The thought has occurred to me a couple of times that the name "Datchery" might be an echo of Pondicherry, the French colony in India.

SPY SERIES CHARACTERS IN HARDBACK, III
By Barry Van Tilburg

DOSSIER #19: Dorian Silk.
CREATED BY: Simon Harvester.
OCCUPATION: Agent for British Intelligence
ASSOCIATES: Swan (first boss, killed in action), Priest (second and last boss).
WEAPONS: Knives and guns.
OTHER COMMENTS: Works mostly in the middle and far East. Can more or less blend into the background. He was once offered a job back in London but refused; he didn't think he could fit into English society anymore.
Unsung Road (Jarrolds, 1961; Walker, 1961).
Silk Road (Jarrolds, 1962; Walker, 1963).
Red Road (Jarrolds, 1963; Walker, 1964).
Assassins Road (Jarrolds, 1965; Walker, 1965).
Treacherous Road (Jarrolds, 1966; Walker, 1967).
Battle Road (Jarrolds, 1967; Walker, 1968).
Zion Road (Jarrolds, 1968; Walker, 1968).
Nameless Road (Jarrolds, 1969; Walker, 1970).
Moscow Road (Jarrolds, 1970; Walker, 1971).
Sahara Road (Jarrolds, 1972; Walker, 1972).
Forgotten Road (Jarrolds, 1974; Walker, 1974).
Siberian Road (Jarrolds, 1976; Walker, 1976).

DOSSIER #20: Dr. Jason Love.
CREATED BY: James Leasor.
OCCUPATION: Full time doctor and part time agent of British Intelligence.
ASSOCIATES: MacGillivray, his boss.
WEAPONS: Hates them, but can use them.
OTHER COMMENTS: Love has a way of running into espionage plots. He has an affinity for old cars and owns a Cord. David Niven played Love in a movie called *Where the Spies Are*, based on *Passport to Oblivion*, in which Love stumbles onto an assassination plot.
Passport to Oblivion (Heinemann, 1964; Lippincott, 1965).
Passport to Peril (Heineman, 1966; published as *Spylight* by Putnam, 1967).
Passport in Suspense (Heineman, 1967; published as *The Yang Meridian* by Putnam, 1968).
Passport for a Pilgrim (Heinemann, 1968; Doubleday, 1969).
A Week of Love (Heinemann, 1969).
Love All (Heinemann, 1971).
Love and the Land Beyond (Heinemann, 1979).

DOSSIER #21: Dr. David Grant.
CREATED BY: George B. Mair.
OCCUPATION: Agent for a NATO department called SHAPE.
ASSOCIATES: Admiral Cooper, his boss; Krystelle de Tourvell, his girlfriend and fellow agent.
WEAPONS: .357 magnum, poison ring, gas pellets.
OTHER COMMENTS: Grant is one of the most violent agents in the genre. Developed his own gas pellets and poison ring. His adversary in the first half of the series is an organization called SATAN. In the first book Grant helps a

Russian ballerina to defect and gets back at the KGB for trying to mess up his life.
Death's Foot Forward (Jarrolds, 1963; Random, 1964).
Miss Torquoise (Jarrolds, 1964; Random, 1965).
Live, Love, and Cry (Jarrolds, 1965; John Day, 1965).
Kisses from Satan (Jarrolds, 1966; John Day, 1966).
The Girl from Peking (Jarrolds, 1967; John Day, 1967).
Black Champagne (Jarrolds, 1968; John Day, 1968).
Goddesses Never Die (Jarrold, 1969).
A Wreath of Camellias (Jarrolds, 1970).
Crimson Jade (Jarrolds, 1971).
Paradise Spells Danger (Jarrolds, 1973).

DOSSIER #22: Simon Bognor.
CREATED BY: Tim Heald.
OCCUPATION: Board of Trade (Special Investigations Department), where he dabbles in customs and espionage.
ASSOCIATES: Parkinson (his boss), Monica (his lady).
WEAPONS: Violence seems to make him nauseated.
OTHER COMMENTS: Books often have violent endings, but they are not really brought about by Bognor. Bognor likes to eat, and he hates his boss.
Unbecoming Habits (Hutchinson, 1973; Stein & Day, 1973).
Blue Blood Will Out (Hutchinson, 1974; Stein & Day, 1974).
Deadline (Hutchinson, 1975).
Let Sleeping Dogs Die (Hutchinson, 1976).
Just Deserts (Hutchinson, 1977).

DOSSIER #23: Paul Kilgerrin.
CREATED BY: Charles Leonard (M.V. Heberden).
OCCUPATION: A private eye who works part time as an agent of American Military Intelligence.
ASSOCIATES: Gol. Mathewson (his boss), Gerry Cordent (his girlfriend and helper).
WEAPONS: Kilgerrin is a sharpshooter and a quick draw artist who can also use and throw a knife.
OTHER COMMENTS: Kilgerrin is a last chance man. He gets dumped into situations where other agents before him have died or turned up missing. The opposition expects another agent but not a shady private investigator. Kilgerrin, like Joe Gall, almost dies in the end of the books. In the first book Kilgerrin goes looking for a saboteur in an airplane factory during WWII.
Deadline for Destruction (Doubleday, 1942).
The Stolen Squadron (Doubleday, 1942).
The Fanatic of Fez (Doubleday, 1943).
The Secret of the Spa (Doubleday, 1944).
Expert in Murder (Doubleday, 1945).
Pursuit in Peru (Doubleday, 1946).
Search for a Scientist (Doubleday, 1947).
The Fourth Funeral (Doubleday, 1948).
Sinister Shelter (Doubleday, 1949).
Secrets for Sale (Doubleday, 1950).
Treachery in Trieste (Doubleday, 1951)

IT'S ABOUT CRIME
By Marvin Lachman

Still they come, the progeny of Sherlock Holmes, spinning off their way into our book stores. They might be giants like *The Seven Per Cent Solution* or at least legitimate like the Solar Pons stories; they might be bastards. According to my recollection (and *The Encyclopedia Sherlockiana* by Jack Tracy), chess is never mentioned in the canon. Yet, in *The Chess Mysteries of Sherlock Holmes* (Alfred A. Knopf, 171 pp., $10.00), mathematician-logician Raymond Smullyan has invented fifty chess problems which he recounts within the context of brief Holmes-Watson narratives. There are even ten problems created by Professor Moriarty. The problems range from relatively easy (as Holmes instructs Watson in the game) to the difficult. It's more for the chess player than for the mystery reader, but is a delight for the person who enjoys both. And who says you can't love a bright child born out of "headlock."

There have been too few general histories of the mystery story. While Leroy Lad Panek's *Watteau's Shepherds* (Bowling Green University Popular Press, 232 pp., $13.95 hardcover, $5.95 paperback) only covers the detective novel in Britain between the World Wars, it is the best thing to come along since Haycraft's *Murder for Pleasure*. Incidentally, the unusual title derives from the Graves-Hodge analogy of the detective story being as unrealistic as the shepherds painted by Watteau, the 18th Century French artist. Panek's viewpoint is one to which I subscribe. We read the mystery itself, and about it, not for any dry academic reason, but rather because of the intelligent escape to be found in "the quiet laughs and quaint complexities of a good detective story."

In chapters about Bentley, Christie, Milne, Sayers, Cox, Allingham, Carr, and Marsh, Panek traces the roots of the Golden Age detective novel to the "thriller" and shows how it evolved into the puzzle. In each case he effectively captures the essence of the writer he discusses. He also nicely disposes of Chandler's myth that realism is necessary for a good detective story. Realism is only necessary for reality, not for escape.

This book is remarkably error-free, except for rare lapses like the spelling of Carroll John Daly. Panek has a good way with a phrase, e.g., "Agatha Troy is Harriet Vane in a painter's smock." I also like his acknowledgment of the problems of writing *about* the mystery without discussing the ending as making detective criticism into "an exercise in ingenuity like the detective story itself." Well done, Mr. Panek. *Watteau's Shepherds* is both informative and enjoyable, an unbeatable combination.

Two outstanding short story anthologies have been published recently. In *The Edgar Winners* (Random House, 420 pp., $11.95) Bill Pronzini has selected a generous share of the short stories awarded the MWA "Edgar." (Where an author received the prize for his total work or for a collection, Pronzini has selected a representative story.) My favorites among the 24 stories are:

Philip MacDonald, "Love Lies Bleeding," 1952
Roald Dahl, "Lamb to the Slaughter," 1953
Stanley Ellin, "The Blessington Method," 1956
Lawrence Treat, "H as in Homicide," 1964
Thomas Walsh, "Chance after Chance," 1977

Pronzini also includes a list of *all* Edgar winners (in all categories) since they began. Has anyone else noted that, in addition to being one of the best writers of the Private Eye story, Bill Pronzini has become one of our most imaginative editors?

Ballantine's *Verdict of 13* is a paperback reprint of a 1978 anthology of London's Detection Club and what a collection it is! Included are Dick Francis, Michael Gilbert, Patricia Highsmith, H.R.F. Keating, Christianna Brand, Michael Innes, Peter Dickinson, and Julian Symons. There is also "Morepork" by Ngaio Marsh, one of her few works not about Roderick Alleyn. On the other hand, there is P.D. James' "Great-Aunt Allie's Flypapers," the first Adam Dalgliesh short story.

Future historians may look back on the early 1980's as one of the Golden Ages of the series detective. After fifteen years in which the creations of Gardner, Christie, Fleming, and Spillane took up a disproportionate amount of the paperback shelf space, we are getting more variety. The numbers are greater than I can keep up with, but it is a pleasure to see my "must read" pile grow.

Charter, which rescued *The Floating Admiral*, deserves top honors for quantity, quality, and variety. They are giving us many of the Saint novels of Leslie Charteris, including the very first in the series, *Meet the Tiger* (1928), out of print for at least a decade. They have spanned thirty years in publishing three fine Gideon Fell novels by John Dickson Carr: *The Three Coffins* (1935), *He Who Whispers* (1946), and *The House at Satan's Elbow* (1965). I like thee, Doctor Fell, and I know why. Your creator had a sense of humor, explains the fantastic rationally, and raises my hackles with his atmosphere of a thunderstorm always about to break loose.

For those who like the literate English detective story, there is Elizabeth Lemarchand's *Death of an Old Girl* (1967) which has many things to recommend it including a well-described girls' school, a crime map, and a good series detective: Inspector (later Superintendent) Tom Pollard.

Another tradition of the genre is the clergyman detective, and Ralph McInerny's Father Dowling is the latest to follow in the footsteps of Father Brown. Charter has published Dowling's first four adventures: *Her Death of Cold* (1977), *The Seventh Station* (1977), *Bishop as Pawn* (1978), and *Lying Three* (1979).

A nice assortment, and I haven't even mentioned other Charter big guns like Victor Canning, Nick Carter, Donald Westlake, and John Creasey.

Pocket Books, Inc., which started it all in this country in 1939, is still very much with us. They have just published the latest John Putnam Thatcher of Emma Lathen, the very timely, *Double, Double, Oil and Trouble* (1978). They also publish all of Dick Francis, including *Odds Against* (1965), simply one of the best suspense novels ever written. It features ex-jockey Sid Halley who became a series character as a result of *Whip Hand*, Francis's latest, a recent best seller in hardcover.

Jove reaches back to 1940 to reprint Ngaio Marsh's *Death at the Bar*. Those of you who like to think of series characters as old friends will especially enjoy the relationship between Roderick Alleyn and Inspector "Br'er" Fox in this book which is set at a Devonshire pub.

Bantam has taken over the Luis Mendoza books of Dell Shannon, with *Streets of Death* (1976) and *Felony at Random* (1979). If there is one thing that Shannon-Linington will deserve to be remembered for, it is her ability to portray the victim as a human being about whom we care. Would that she could do that with her detectives. Bantam is also publishing the underrated Catherine Aird with *The Religious Body* (1966) and *The Stately Home Murder* (1969), about Inspector Sloan. I hope they'll get to *A Late Phoenix* (1970), the best Aird I've read so far. Also, Bantam has dragged in by her knitting yarn that deceptively soft spinster detective, Miss Maud Silver, in Patricia Wentworth's *The Listening Eye* (1955) and *The Fingerprint* (1956).

And if that is not enough variety, there is more. Berkeley is publishing the novels of Rex Burns about Gabe Wager of the Denver P.D., *The Farnsworth Score* (1977) and *Speak for the Dead* (1978). They also do Simon Brett's series about Charles Paris, who is a better detective than he is an actor. *An Amateur Corpse* (1978) is the latest in the series.

Writers have always sought to make their series characters unusual. Few are more so that George C. Chesbro's Dr. Robert Frederickson, better known as "Mongo," a dwarf detective with a Ph.D. in Criminology and a black belt in karate. Don't be put off for this is a highly-praised, fast- paced series of three books so far, all published by Signet: *Shadow of a Broken Man* (1977), *City of Whispering Stone* (1978), and *An Affair of Sorcerers* (1979).

I have just scratched the surface of what is available. I don't want to hear anyone complaining they haven't got a thing to read.

LESLIE CHARTERIS AND THE SAINT
Five Decades of Partnership

By Jan Alexandersson and Iwan Hedman
(Translated and edited by Carl Larsen)

Those who claim that truth is stranger than fiction have an excellent example in the creator of Simon Templar, alias the Saint. One of our time's great adventurers and bon vivants, he was born into an ancient royal family whose roots can be traced back over 3,700 years. Never having to work for a living, he nonetheless amassed a fortune through his own efforts. His name is Leslie Charteris. But let us begin at the beginning.

Leslie Charles Bowyer Yin was born in Singapore on May 12, 1907. He is Anglo-Chinese: his mother English, his father a member of the Yin family who were emperors of China during the Shang dynasty (1760-1120 B.C.). Dr. S. C. Yin was a well-known surgeon, director of several companies and member of some of the most exclusive clubs in Singapore. Leslie grew up on fashionable Leonie Drive in a mansion staffed by Chinese and Malay servants; thus, he spoke these languages even before learning the English alphabet.

When he did begin to read English, he read what all boys of that era read first: the weekly boys' magazines such as *Chums*. Although those remained his favorites, his reading soon advanced to Robin Hood and other tales of adventure. Beginning to dream of travel and adventure, he provided an outlet for his fantasies by starting his own magazine. Typing each copy separately, he wrote poems and stories, and drew the illustrations. Finding himself weak at drawing human figures, he solved the problem by simplifying them to matchstick figures. Young Leslie sold the magazine to relatives and friends of the family. He endeared himself to those who did not at first wish to subscribe by blackmailing them. Many years later, of course, the matchstick figures reappeared when Charteris sought an identifying symbon for the Saint. Simon Templar's calling card became the haloed stick figure.

If Leslie Charteris' ancestry is remarkable, his upbringing was no less so. Provided with a governess and a tutor, he had several times travelled around the world with his parents before he was twelve. He was given a taste of authentic adventure in 1914 when World War I broke out. He was aboard a ship in the Mediterranean which was intercepted by a German warship. After German soldiers boarded and seized a passenger, the ship was then permitted to continue its course towards Egypt and the Suez Canal.

After the war, when Leslie was twelve, his father decided that the time had come for him to receive the benefits of an English education. Leslie objected that he was not particularly interested and that he could learn much more without formal schooling. These objections were to no avail.

After finishing prep school at Falconhurst, Purley, Leslie was sent to the Rossall School at Fleetwood in Lancastershire. He did not take great pains keeping up with the curriculum in his four years there, devoting most of his time to the student publications. He also took the time to do a great deal of reading, going through such authors as Conan Doyle, Sapper, Dumas, Edgar Wallace and R. Austin Freeman. These all shaped his desire to become an author himself when his schooling was over. Although at this time he felt that Freeman's Dr. Thorndyke was much more the model for a scientific detective than Doyle's Holmes, Charteris later came to be an expert on the latter through his collaboration with Denis Green on the scripts for the famous radio series in which Basil Rathbone played Holmes to Nigel Bruce's Dr. Watson. Charteris, under the name Bruce Taylor, created the plots while Green dramatized them. This team produced over 70 scripts, including cases to which Doyle referred but never chronicled. Thus, Leslie Charteris actually came to produce more adventures of Sherlock Holmes than did Sir Arthur Conan Doyle.

Of course, these accomplishments were still far in the future, but Leslie Yin gave an indication of what was to come when he sold his first story at 16. The story, which brought him only a few guineas, has unfortunately not survived.

Finishing school at Rossall in 1924, he moved to Paris to continue his studies. Making no giant strides there, he returned to England the following year. There, despite his lack of serious academic ambitions, he entered Cambridge. Not surprisingly, he found that Greek and Latin were not his cup of tea.

He then wrote another story which was published in *Sovereign Magazine* in January 1925. The story, "One Crowded Hour," was published under the name of Leslie C. Bowyer (Bowyer was his mother's maiden name). This and other stories which he sold in 1925 under the names Leslie C. Bowyer and L. Charles Bowyer were only modestly remunerated, but the fact of their publication served as a definite spur.

So, after one year at Cambridge, Leslie wrote his father that he was planning to leave school for good and become an author.

Dr. Yin was furious: he had intended Leslie to take over his practice. When Leslie's determination held fast, Dr. Yin determined that Leslie would get no further financial assistance from his parents.

Thus when he came down from Cambridge Leslie Yin was nineteen, with no degree, no trade and no hope yet of being able to support himself completely by writing. Wanderlust took hold and like the heroes in the romances he had read, he went out into the world to seek his fortune, changing his name to Leslie Charteris in the process. He wound up in Southeast Asia as a gold prospector in the Malayan jungles. After fishing for pearls and working in a tin mine, he had saved just enough to finance a return trip to England. There he supported himself through such jobs as tending bar and professional bridge playing.

Through all of this, he kept on writing and began to sell steadily. Ward, Lock and Co., Ltd., published three novels. The first, *X Esquire*, was published in England in 1927. Before the second appeared, he had a short story, "Bright Young People," published in *Pall Mall Magazine* for January, 1928. Novel number two, *The White Rider*, was brought out in 1928. *Pall Mall* published another short story, "The Man Who Was Arrogant," in July 1928. Then, that September, Ward,

Lock issued the third of Charteris' novels, *Meet the Tiger*. This was the first story in which Simon Templar, alias the Saint, appeared. None of these three novels caused any big stir, either with the public or the critics. Of course, no one had any idea of what the future would bring, nor had the publishers beaten the publicity drums for a completely unknown author.

In January 1929, Ward Lock issued Charteris' fourth book, a non-Saint effort called *Daredevil*. In August, Amalgamated Press reprinted *Meet the Tiger* in The Boys' Friends Library under the title of *Crooked Gold*. Regarding "Leslie Charteris" as something less than a household word, they omitted mention of any author's name at all.

During this year Charteris had successfully linked up with the Amalgamated Press, which was starting a new periodical, *The Thriller*. This weekly came gradually to play a major role for him and he continued to write for it until its demise with the World War II paper shortages. The first story in what was to be a long series was "The Story of a Dead Man" on March 2, 1929. Later that year, in seven installments, the *Empire News*, a Sunday newspaper, published a novel which Charteris christened *The Black Cat*. That became the last novel of his which Ward, Lock brought out, changing the title to *The Bandit* in the process.

The Thriller first published "The Five Kings" on May 4, 1929. Charteris later rewrote it as "The Man Who Was Clever" and rechristened the main characters. Their original names were drawn from a deck of playing cards: the four kings and the joker. The joker of course became Simon Templar whose initials--S.T.--obviously led to his canonization. The logo of the original gang was five cards: four kings with the joker in the center. From there it's only a short step to the stick figure with the halo. Charteris used the same technique on other *Thriller* stories to give them a saintly cast.

In the early stages of the Saint's career, Charteris enlisted many persons to help out in different Saintly endeavors. Many of these were modeled on friends of the author. Of course there was the blonde, blue-eyed girl who was at the Saint's side in so many adventures: Patricia Holm. Among the merry men were Monty Hayward (based on the editor of *The Thriller*, Montague Hayden), Roger Conway, Dickie Tremayne, Terry Mannering, Archie Sheriden, Hoppy Uniatz, Sam Outrell and larst, but not least, 'Orace. These formed the Saint's organization of merry, free and fearless adventurers. In later years, these recede into the background as the Saint becomes more and more of a solo act.

On the other side of the law there was first Scotland Yard's Chief inspector Claude Eustace Teal, whose gumchewing proclivities enriched the Wrigley family fortunes. When the Saint changed his venue to America, Charteris provided him with another guardian of the law to torment: Inspector John Henry Fernack of the New York City Police Department.

In 1930, Charteris changed publishers, going from Ward, Lock to Hodder and Stoughton, where he got better terms as well as the possibility of a larger audience. The first book which they published in May 1930, *The Last Hero*, is an example of how Charteris joined different stories to form a novel. *The Thriller* story, "Sudden Death," November 9, 1929, makes up the middle section while "The Creeping Death," July 7, 1929, serves as the first and last quarters of the novel. Now, relatively well-established as an author, Charteris devoted time to studying subjects which had not been in the Cambridge curriculum: jurisprudence and criminology.

In 1932 he contracted with the *Empire News* to supply a weekly story featuring the Saint. Some of these written then, such as "The Whipping of Titus Oakes," are generally considered the best Charteris ever produced. Hodder and Stoughton collected these twenty-five stories in *The Brighter Buccaneer* (1933) and *Boodle* (1934).

Despite these successes, financial security was still not assured. The urge to travel gripped Charteris again and he left England to try his luck in America. After arriving, he began to write immediately and sold a Saint story for $400, quite a large sum then and considerably more than he could hope to earn on the English market. Going to Hollywood, he also wrote film scripts, among them the George Raft film *Midnight Club*. Before long he was getting $1,000 a story. This was the consummation which he had devoutly wished: now for the first time in his life he could live in the style he wished and save money at the same time.

During 1934-36 Charteris also produced plots for the comic strip *Secret Agent X-9* which had been created by Dashiell Hammett. The artist for this strip was Alex Raymond who also created *Rip Kirby* and then went on to intergalactic glory with *Flash Gordon*.

In 1938 RKO contracted to capture the Saint on celluloid. Planning a series, they selected one of the better full-length books to start: *The Saint in New York* (1935). RKO staked a great deal of money on the project. Louis Hayward, known for his swashbuckling roles, was chosen for the role of the Saint.

Although the film critics in general were hardly enthusiastic, they did not pan the film. Thanks to this, RKO went ahead with the series, but some retrenching led to George Sanders taking over the Simon Templar role.

This casting was successful; tall, suave and well able to project menace, for over twenty years Sanders was considered the most effective film actor to portray the Saint. His first appearance was in *The Saint Strikes Back* (1938), adapted from the novel *She Was a Lady* (1931). His second effort was *The Saint in London* (1939). Taken from the short story "The Million Pound Note" in *The Holy Terror* (1932), this is often regarded as the best motion picture made from the Saint stories. Sanders wore the halo in three more films, all based on unpublished stories by Charteris. They were *The Saint's Double Trouble* (1940), *The Saint Takes Over* (1940), and *The Saint in Palm Springs* (1941).

RKO then cast Sanders as the Falcon in films bearing a striking resemblance to those based on Charteris' creation. In fact, many felt that the Falcon films were nothing but a rip-off of the Saint. Charteris won a settlement supporting this view, but Hollywood and the Saint were through for a while.

British stage actor Hugh Sinclair took the halo for two films made in England: *The Saint's Vacation* (1941), a revision of *Getaway* (1932), and *The Saint Meets the Tiger* (1943), springing from the first Saint book. Louis Hayward had a last fling in *The Saint's Girl Friday* (1954), an adaptation of "The Spanish War" from *The Ace of Knaves* (1937). Two French versions, *Le Saint Mene La Danse* (1960) and *Le Saint Prend l'Affut* (1966), could perhaps be best described as "les miserables." Charteris therefore refused to permit any further celluloid desecration of the Saintly canon.

Both Saint fans and Leslie Charteris had trouble in seeing any of these actors as the perfect screen incarnation of Simon Templar. Charteris' on choice would have been Cary Grant. Unhappily, this desire was never realized.

In other media, others took the Templar role. *Life* of May 19, 1941, offered a pictorial feature in celebration of the mystery story's centennial. Through the photos and text, the reader was given all the clues and challenged to solve a mystery. The Saint was portrayed by none other than Leslie Charteris, monocle and all. This story became "Palm Springs" in *The Saint Goes West* (1942).

Nineteen-forty-five found the Saint on the radio in the U.S.A. Saint aficionados were more generally pleased with the radio version than with the films. Freed from the need of finding someone who looked like the Saint, the producers found many suitable voices. The stories stayed closer to the originals as well. During the Saint's run on radio, the Templar role was assumed by several actors: Edgar Barrier, Brian Aherne, Barry Sullivan, Tom Conway, and today's master of horror, Vincent Price.

Charteris next launched the Saint as a comic strip, writing the plots himself; *The New York Herald Tribune* syndicated the popular strip which appeared in many newspapers, as well as leading to a Saint comic book. Charteris produced the strip for ten years, during which time it appeared daily. During this time, understandably, there were few new Saint books. Charteris did, however, write articles on food and leisure.

Having lived in America for many years, Leslie Charteris qualified for American citizenship, which he took out on July 27, 1946.

The Saint Mystery Magazine made its debut in 1953 on a bi-monthly basis and was so well-received that it quickly became a monthly, running until 1967. From issue to issue "old" Saint stories would alternate with new ones. Crime writers of the past and present provided the other stories. Hans Stefan Santesson, considered one of the top pros in the business, did the managing editorial work. There was eventually a British edition, as well as French and Dutch versions. Charteris contributed a monthly editorial word; toward the end of the run he would write essays on whatever topic took his fancy.

In the sixties, the Saint became even more famous, reaching an even larger audience than previously. The tabloids headlined the news that the Saint was to become a TV series. The plots would come from the original stories, but the big question was, who would be right for the role of the Saint? Many entertainment columnists speculated, some offering the usual inside tips. Charteris, after seeing the last few films, was understandably apprehensive. A strong candidate was Patrick McGoohan, well known from such TV series as "The Prisoner" and "Secret Agent," but he lost out, the producers felling that he lacked the necessary light touch.

After many months of searching, the halo was awarded to

Roger Moore, who had the right height, physique and looks. He also possessed the necessary Saintly carefree spirit and wit. Born in London, he spoke English with no noticeable regional accent, a definite plus since the show was to be aimed at an international market. He also was a sports car driver and a globetrotter who spoke French, German and Italian.

Everything started to fall into place and the first episode, "The Talented Husband," was telecast on September 19, 1962. Immediate reaction, while favorable, was not overwhelming, but as the series continued, the public became more and more fond of it, and soon it was a hit. The first season, originally planned for 26 episodes, was expanded to 39. That first season was followed by several others from which some adventures were released in motion picture form. Roger Moore had become the Saint; it was hard to imagine anyone else in the role.

The majority of the critics filed favorable reports, finding the show quite entertaining. Naturally, adverse critics emerged, but these were mainly of the highbrow persuasion, regarding the show as mere entertainment with no redeeming social values. This type of negative criticism had been anticipated by Charteris and all connected with the show. They brushed it away, knowing that in many countries viewers from nine to ninety found that watching the Saint defeat the Ungodly provided a truly enjoyable hour.

There was a total of 120 episodes, most based on original stories. In the last seasons, however, shows were written from plots suggested or approved by Charteris. These stories were edited and published as *The Saint on TV* (1968), *The Saint Returns* (1969), and *The Saint and the Fiction Makers* (1970). After their original run on NBC in the U.S.A., the shows went into syndication. In the summer of 1980 CBS brought them back, making "The Saint" the only TV show ever to return to a major network after being syndicated.

Leslie Charteris' character seems destined for immortality, rivaled perhaps only by Sherlock Holmes for longevity and popularity.

Who served as the model for the Saint? That Leslie Charteris took himself as the model there can be no serious doubt. Although he has at times denied it, at other times he has explained that he could be the Saint's inferior twin brother. There are many striking similarities. Both Leslie Charteris and the Saint dress elegantly and are adventuresome. Both have the same physique, same height and the same black hair, brushed back. Both sported monocles at one time, Charteris proving he was the Saint's equal by keeping his in place while riding a bucking bronco. Both are skilled swimmers, skin-divers and spearfishermen. Both are skilled pilots, rated for several types of flying. Both are skilled marksmen and knifethrowers; although no real person could match the skill at knifethrowing attributed to the Saint, Charteris is no slouch at the sport either. Both speak many languages fluently, among them English, German, Spanish and French. Charteris has even written a textbook, *Spanish for Fun*. Both believe that the good life consists in eating well, drinking well and loafing.

To conclude this essay tracing Leslie Charteris and the Saint over five decades, we will quote the apt words of the

Swedish critic Bo Lundin:

> The charm of the books lies in the exhilarating writing style and the nonchalant superman pose. Nothing is impossible for the Saint and he greets death rays and pistol muzzles with the same polite interest and outrageously flippant repartee. Charteris has succeeded in combining the undeniable charm of his hero with a menace underneath the surface, an undertone of competence and skill that is never allowed to get the upper hand, but is always there.

The Saint goes marching on!

EDITOR'S NOTE: This article, superbly translated by Carl Larsen, is the biographical section of *Leslie Charteris och Helgonet under 5 decennier: en Bio-Bibliografi*, published as DAST Dossier #2 by DAST Förlag AB, Strängnäs, 1973. In one of the letters Carl wrote to me regarding this article--which has been in the works for some time--he says, "If you do publish this opus, perhaps it would be appropriate for you to mention that Iwan still has these books available and that, with this portion Elglished, the rest, consisting of bibliography, filmography and illustrations, would be pretty easy to deal with as the English titles of the books and stories are used, as well as the Swedish ones for those translated." I don't know the price--perhaps Iwan will tell us in a letter next issue--but Iwan's address is: Iwan Hedman, Flodins Väg 5, S-152 00 Strängnäs, Sweden.

THE GREAT MERLINI
By Fred Dueren

The recorded case of Clayton Rawson's Merlini are few, four novels and a handful of short stories, all recorded by his friend Ross Harte. They are in a unique category because each of them is tightly woven around magic, ghosts and psychic happenings. Dr. Gideon Fell often solved cases that had a supernatural element, a tinge of wierd, evil forces. Merlini's cases lack the thrill of malevolence but carry the fascination of seeing a woman cut in half, or a three-ton elephant disappear. In fact, "Nothing Is Impossible" is Merlini's trademark and slogan, hung predominently on the wall in his shop.

Merlini was born in a circus car somewhere in Illinois. He was "the black sheep of the family of Riding Merlinis, ace circus equestrians for five generations. Spending all of his practice time as a boy in the company of the sideshow magician, he dealt a nearly mortal blow to the family pride when he failed to master the back somersault from horse to horse. From the first the acrobatics that fascinated him were the subtler nimble-fingered ones of sleight-of-hand." His first stage work was in the circus at the age of three when he was outfitted as a Nubian. As a final testimony to his inherited place in the circus world is the fact that his godfather was P. T. Barnum. His active career, however, began as a sideshow sorcerer. Somewhere along the way he also picked up talent as an adept pickpocket.

Although he moved away from circus life he never completely deserted it. Whenever a circus came within 100 miles of New York City, Merlini would be there. "Merlini, with all that pink lemonade running in his veins and circus performers swinging from every branch of his family tree, reverts to type every spring."

Just as we never learn Merlini's first name (the initial is A), we also learn very little of his early years or the years when he established his reputation. That he was well-known and made extensive tours is beyond doubt. We do know that he was in London in 1915. While performing at the Palladium, a run cut short by a Zepplin dropping a bomb on his hotel and leaving a splinter in his arm, Merlini was also a member of the London Psychical Society and was doing some work on one of their investigating committees. In *No Coffin for a Corpse* (1942) Harte tells us that Merlini's farewell tour was in 1929, after 26 years of entertaining in circuses and theaters. But that was only the end of one career; Merlini went on to become an author, a magic trick retailer, a psychic investigator, and a Broadway producer, as well as a detective.

Merlini did not look like a magician, according to Harte. He was tall, on the lean side, with black twinkling eyes and black hair. His face appears rather lopsided due to a smile that crinkled around one side of his mouth and an ear that stuck out farther than the other. He's also noted for the graceful, "utterly confident way he carried himself" and the quick, fluid movements of his hands. His clothes vary from impeccable neatness to "slack" and "disoriented", but either way his pockets are stuffed with miscellaneous magic gadgets. "Merlini likes surf bathing, table tennis, puzzles, Times Square and Mrs. Merlini. He can smell any circus that approaches within a radius of 100 miles, and he promptly disappears in that direction. He dislikes subways, beer, inactivity, grand opera and golf." There are a few other references to Mrs. Merlini, but she never appears in the stories. She's always at home (13½ Washington Square North) or out of town visiting relatives while Merlini and Harte are on their adventures.

After his retirement from the stage Merlini's talent and time went mostly into running the Magic Shop, on the top floor of an old building at 1479 Broadway, near Times Square. On the frosted glass panel of the door is painted "The Magic Shop--Miracles for Sale--A. Merlini, Prop." Inside, the right wall is covered with framed and autographed pictures of famous magicians, and playbills of their performances. On the left is Merlini's collection of circus posters. The back wall is covered with shelves of magic paraphernalia and the cash register, above which is lettered "Nothing Is Impossible." Incongruously, the top shelf holds a brightly painted set of Punch and Judy figures. Behind the counter is a door to the office and back room where Merlini designs and manufactures the equipment for larger illusions and special orders. He keeps a white rabbit as the Shop's mascot, feeding it with carrots stored in the cash register. In *Death From a Top Hat* (1938), Hart also reports that the Shop houses a black cat, Dr. Faustus, but he does not appear in the later books.

Since much of Merlini's time must be spent outside the Shop to fulfill all his other interests, he hired another magician, Guy Fawkes, as an assistant. Fawkes was "an odd little Believe-It-Or-Not sort of man with a long face, a wide grin, and a remarkable body.... In his younger days as a carnival controtionist he was billed as TWISTO--The Man Who Turns Himself Inside Out." Magicians and conjurers of all sorts congregate at the Shop. It was "a shop that is somehow all at once gay, festive, bizarre, spectacular, weird, showey, and comfortable." But the skulls and black magic equipment also give it "a distinct air of sulphur and brimstone."

Closely related to magic, Merlini's second greatest interest seems to have been in ghosts, spirits, and exposing fake psychic phenomena. It was because of his expertise in spiritualism and the occult that Harte and Inspector Gavigan decided to call him in for help in *Death from a Top Hat*. His plans to be the emcee of a radio program, "The Ghost Hour", to be broadcast from various haunted houses, led him to Skelton Island in *Footprints on the Ceiling* (1939). In addition to being a member of the London Psychical Society, he is the chairman of the *American Scientist* psychic investigating committee. Due largely to Merlini's work, the committee's standing challenge of being able to reproduce any psychic occurrence withstood any attempts to win the $10,000 challenge money. He subscribed to the *Journal of Parapsychology* and of course was familiar with all the known psychics and mediums, such as Colonel Watrouss and Madame Rappourt, who appear in two of the novels.

As all connoisseurs do, he sometimes got carried away with his subject. "Merlini, once started on a history of magic, either black or white, was all too likely to deliver an oration that carried it in extensive detail right on up to the present day, with an added appendix of predictions as to its future." Not only magic will tempt him to speeches-- at times Merlini has given lectures of varying length on catalepsy and being buried alive, circus acts and performers, locked-room mysteries, the theory of deception and misdirection, witchcraft, and the specialized slang of hoboes and circus people.

It was sometimes easier for Merlini's audience to listen to these lectures than it is to read them. His voice was "richly resonant" with "an unusual range of depth and tone." Harte occasionally got exasperated with Merlini's own form of manipulation and described his voice and speeches as an "almost hypnotic voice that with deft, unnoticed misdirection propels you along an apparently sound but quite illogical path of thought, and then with no warning, springs a trap door that leaves you standing on the sheer edge of an impossibility." When Harte is more charitable he states that Merlini's speech is usually dry, ironic and humorous, his voice one that "could sell you anything."

It is only through Ross Harte's eyes that we see Merlini. How they originally met is unclear. They are always good friends, but they lack the intimacy of many detective pairs. There seem to be periods between cases where they see little of each other. But as the series progresses these periods decline.

Harte maintains his own apartment at 742 East 40th Street (once it is given as East 41st Street). Even though the murder in *Death from a Top Hat* occurs in the apartment across the hall from him, we see little of Harte's rooms or private life. As a recorder of Merlini's cases, Harte does a fairly thorough job of not intruding in the story. Not until the last book, *No Coffin for the Corpse*, does his life effect the telling. And then it is because his involvement with Kathryn Wolff brings him head-on into a murder at the Wolff mansion.

Harte is a professional writer. His work varies from newspaper reporter, to free-lance advertising with Blanton, Dunlop and Hartwick, to magazine articles (in *Top Hat* he is working on an article on the state of the modern detective story, to be titled something like "Death is Hackneyed" or "The Corpse on the Publisher's Hands"), to ghosting a history of the fashion industry. He has apparently written some detective stories (Merlini implies he wrote them for the pulps) and then began writing up Merlini's cases, in a collaborative effort with him. Harte had the contract to do the writing, but he'd have Merlini go over the proofs to be sure the details and mechanics of the crime were correct. In *Footprints* Harte was also working on a Braodway revue, but whether as a writer for the show itself or as an advertising/publicity man is a bit unclear. Later, when Merlini is putting together his own magical, musical revue, "Hocus Pocus", at the Drury Lane Theater, Harte is out of a job and hired by Merlini to do the show's publicity.

Otherwise there's little to say about Harte. He drinks scotch and black coffee and smokes. He brings a couple of cases to Merlini's attention but does little investigation or detective work on them himself. Merlini says he has a romantic nature. He is fairly adept at photography and does his own developing. At the end of *Coffin* there is a strong implication that he will marry Kathryn Wolff--after all he had asked her and was planning on it until her father and murder stepped in.

The official arm of Merlini's investigations is Inspector Homer Gavigan, "one of the department's brighter lights." Due to Merlini's giving some lectures and demonstrations at the police college on the tricks of card sharps and con men, Gavigan knew him before that first case. In fact, both Harte and Gavigan had been thinking of calling him in to explain some of the occult and magical elements of the murder. Gavigan is short, having just reached minimum height for the force. He seems somewhere in his mid-forties, but it is never specified. Beside the fact that he is married and has "frosty blue eyes," we know very little about him. We do know that he dislikes fanciness and tricks mixed with his crime (all those things that make cases appealing to Merlini) so he acts frustrated and short-tempered in the bizarre impossibilities he encounters. He is "a hard-headed skeptic."

In *The Headless Lady* (1940) one other character of interest appears--mystery writer Stuart Towne. Since Clayton Rawson used that pseudonym himself to write several mysteries, it is tantalizing to speculate how much Towne equals Rawson. In *Lady* Towne is spending two weeks with the circus to get background for his next book. He is credited with *The Empty Coffin* and *The Man with the Purple Face*, the cover of which says he is an ex-bank-robber and ex-con-man. He's also written articles for magazines--"The Gentle Art of Safe Cracking," "Con Men I Have Known," and "Hoboes and Their Habits."

Towne is described as a "stoutish" middle-aged man who does not look like an author. He was too ordinary, with a commonplace, trite face hiding a clever, active brain. At first Harte thought he was a colorless drab man, but the longer he knew him the more he seemed to change and it was harder to pin him down. Towne always carries a gun (a suspicious character, indeed!) and claims he has a collection of them at his home in Mamaroneck, New York. He also claims to know a fair amount about codes and ciphers.

Merlini's work as a detective falls squarely in the middle of the Golden Age guidelines. The unusual plots, impossible crimes and locked rooms, and emphasis on puzzle rather than character meet all the conventions. The murder scene is often cut off in some way to eliminate all but a handful of suspects. Merlini's own eccentricities and uniqueness have been noted already. As a detective, Merlini can walk into a room that was supposed to have been locked at the time of the murder, and immediately "see" the solution, the gimmick that was used. His problem, as that of so many amateur detectives, is to get the proof necessary for conviction. Merlini makes a show of playing fair with Harte (the reader) when it comes time to explain. In footnotes he includes page numbers where specific clues or remarks are made. At the time they seemed innocuous enough to the unwary.

Gavigan usually allows Merlini to be present during questionings and to insert his own enquiries. While doing so Merlini abstractly makes coins or lighted matches appear and disappear in his hands. Being a master of illusion and deception he uses these talents in his questioning and outlook on the case. He also uses his ability to pick pockets and locks (he owns a set of picklocks that were once Houdini's). During an investigation he is able to forego sleep completely, leaving Harte dragging behind.

Having such a high energy level, Merlini never seems able to settle down. Instead, he is always dashing off to new projects or conventions, such as the National Convention of Witches, Warlocks, and Banshees, or the Society of American Magicians. He also found time to do some writing, again covering a variety of related themes: *Legerdemaniacs*, *The Psychology of Deception*, and *Sawdust Trails* (about circuses). For sale in the Magic Shop are numerous booklets he has written on particular facets of magic and illusion, such as "Jail, Bank-Vault and Underwater Escapes."

After the four cases and several short adventures, Merlini and Harte disappeared, Harte presumably into marriage and Merlini possibly stepped into one of his magic cabinets and simply never returned.

NOTE: In Anthony Boucher's *Four-and-Twenty Bloodhounds* (1950) Clayton Rawson provided the following biographical sketch. It gives several facts not recorded elsewhere, but the lack of a first name is noticeable.

MERLINI, The Great, magician; b. Barnum & Baily circus car en route through Illinois; s. Victor and Edna (Bradna) M.; educ. at intervals, Ohio, Heidelberg, Brooklyn, Paris, Beirut; m. Mary Cordona, Jan. 2, 1919; children--Michael, 1922, Roberta, 1925. Carnival and circus magician, 1917-20, Keith Circuit, 1921-28, full evening show, 1929-38; world tour, 1935-36; magic dealer, 1939--. Theatrical productions: appeared in *Magic on Broadway, Musical Magic, Impossibly Yours*; produced *Now You See It---*; motion pictures: *Miracles for Sale*; series of short features: *Nothing Is Impossible*; currently starring: *The Great Merlini* television show. Inventor, numerous magic illusions, notably famed Sawing a Woman in Four. Publications: *Legerdemaniacs; The Psychology of Deception; Sleight of Hand for Experts; Magicians of the Underworld*; currently conducts column, "Merlini's Magic," in *Hugard's Magic Monthly*; co-author with Ross Harte under pseudonym Clayton Rawson: *Death from a Top Hat; The Footprints on the Ceiling; The Headless Lady; No Coffin for the Corpse*.

Decorations: Sacred Order of White Elephant, presented at command performance by Maharajah of Saringapatam. Clubs: Society of American Magicians; Circus Fans Club; Lambs Club; Explorers Club; Mystery Writers of America, Inc.; honorary member, N.Y. Homicide Squad; British Magic Circle; Associated Wizards of Aberdeen; Caloutta Conjurers Club; Societe des Prestidigitateurs; Magischer Verein; Gl'Illusionisti; Sociedad de Magia; Banshee Club; Honorary Medicine Man, Bantu Tribe, Lower Congo. Hobbies: Mrs. Merlini; chess; table tennis; firewalking; collecting historical magic apparatus, posters, playbills, books relating to magic, spiritualism, witchcraft. Home address: 13½ Washington Sq. N. Office: The Magic Shop, Times Square. Tel.: MEphisto 7-1313.

MYSTERY*FILE

SHORT REVIEWS BY STEVE LEWIS

Franklin Bandy. *The Blackstock Affair.* Charter 06650-X, 1980, 376 pp., $2.50.

Last year about this time I wrote a review of a book entitled *Deceit and Deadly Lies,* which was the first adventure of Kevin MacInnes, the famous polygraph expert known as the Lie King. It cost $2.25, and my advice, quoted on the back cover of this, the second adventure, was that it was worth the money. Not only that, but it won an Edgar too.

This one will set you back an additional 25¢. It's worth the twenty bits, but gee, I remember when 25¢ was itself the going rate for a paperback. (And everybody knew so well that that's what it was that it wasn't even printed on the front cover.)

Enough of that. The vicissitudes of being a series hero being what they are, in between books MacInnes has lost his wife Vanessa, whom he won only in the final pages of the last adventure, to the vindictive followers of the man he defeated. Ton't feel too sorry for MacInnes, though. He has a new bodyguard-assistant to work for him this time, a former private detective named Amanda Button. In this long, sprawling novel they share some strange adventures together, and I do hope Amanda survives until the next book?

Blackstock, Ohio. The birthrate is dropping without explanation. Not being a medical man, MacInnes ignores all such aspects of the problem, and he aims in instead on what is probably a Commie plot. Or an attack from outer space. Or the machinations of an evil scientist. Or, Ralph Nader would like this one, capitalistic commercial overkill....

Bandy's story-telling style consists of interspersing intelligent commentary on world conditions with tough "masculine" writing--flat declarative sentences and cliffhanger chapter endings. I think he feels obliged to include all the sex and violence that he does as doing what "modern" readers want, but there's such a nervous edge to it, that it seems to me at least that hes' slightly embarrassed by it.

I'm only guessing, of course. Certainly no one should ever knock success. And if action-filled adventure spiced with a modicum of brainwork behind it ever appeals to you at all, don't miss this one. (A minus)

Royce Howes. *The Case of the Copy-Hook Killing.* Dutton, 1945, 223 pp.

Howes started out with a bang as a mystery writer. In the five years between 1935 and 1939 he wrote seven novels, all published by Doubleday and the Crime Club. Then the war came along, and Howes, a newspaperman, did any further writing in the ETO for the Army News Service--information provided, incidentally, by the back flap on the dust jacket. (If you're like me, you'll read anything.)

Both Howes and his leading character, Captain Ben Lucias of the Homicide Squad, returned from the war in 1945. Lucias had been in five of the Crime Club books, but this was the last outing for both of them. Why it was done for Dutton instead of Doubleday, I don't know, but I can guess. As a mystery, it's Not Very Good.

But, a copy-hook? I hear someone asking. A copy-hook is what one of those sharp steel spikes are called that reporters used to use to file their stories on. The scene, naturally enough, is a newspaper office, and it's the reception clerk who's been murdered. He was the guy whose job it was to keep the nuts coming in from the street from off the editors' backs. And so Lucias' ensuing investigation has him busily checking out the crackpots and all the other assorted creeps who saw the dead man last. It's obvious that Howes knew the type well. He laughs at them, and if his characters reflect his own opinions at all, he despises them as much as they do.

What is equally obvious is that the solution to the murder has nothing to do with this list of weirdos that Lucias has to work his way through. But downright distasteful, however, is Captain Lucias' interrogation technique. Slugging a prisoner around in police headquarters is not likely to have been a remarkable occurrence back during the forties, long before today's attempt at enlightened police procedures had begun to make any headway. It's just that it's difficult for me to recall it being done by a series character in police uniform before, one supposedly functioning as a competent detective, as well as one trying to maintain the respect of the reader. (D)

Lesley Andress. *Caper.* Putnam, 1980, 302 pp., $10.95.

Her publisher unhappy about her recent lack-lustre production of mystery thrillers, Jannie Shean, also known as Chuck Thorndyke, Mike Cantrell, and yes, God help us, Brick Wall, among others, faces a crisis in her career. Her books need more reality, she is told. Others tell her they need what you usually don't find happening in real life. Tidy endings, she is advised. No loose ends.

In the pursuit and name of reality, she plans her own crime. A jewel heist, complete with new blonde identity and a crew of several more-than-willing recruits. Events take a sudden expected twist, and she's trapped into pulling it off. The mob gets involved, a dullish sort of book finally becomes exciting, and the chase is on.

Some moralizing about the freedom of amorality and the forced awareness of a life on the run does not cloud the fact that crime is a serious business, and one not entirely suited nor meant for amateurs. No tidy endings here. The story has gone downhill rapidly by book's end. Running out of gas (figuratively) may be the ultimate realism, perhaps, but I've somehow never found it particularly satisfying. (C plus)*
(*Reviews so marked have appeared earlier in the Hartford *Courant*.)

Ellis Peters. *One Corpse Too Many.* Morrow, 1980, 192 pp., $8.95.

For a fine literate change of pace from your standard big-city police procedural or private eye yarn, you could do worse than to try this, the latest mystery adventure to be tackled and solved by the 12th century's answer to Sherlock Holmes, Brother Cadfael of Shrewsbury Abbey.

Stop and think about it. One of the prime requirements of the detective story is that of bringing the murderer to justice, before both God and man. In the year 1138 who else would there be but a devoutly dedicated monk to carry out such a task? Assigned to burial detail after King Stephen's successful siege of the rebellious Castle Foregate, Cadfael discovers that he cannot account for an extra body among those of ninety-four other condemned prisoners. Without a little urging on his part, it couldn't be made more clear that otherwise the distinction between a murder and an execution would have escaped the minds of those in power completely.

The plot is thicker than it seems, romance is determined to bloom even under the worst of conditions, and Cadfael is a solid man of the earth who realizes that God's will may not always be done as honest men would see fit. He makes an ideal detective. (B)

Jonathan Valin. *The Lime Pit.* Dodd, Mead, 1980, 245 pp., $8.95.

Somehow Sherlock Holmes is seldom if ever thought of as a private detective. He seems instead to be intellectually above all that, while of course in reality he was never averse to receiving a fee for his services. And so the fact remains that investigators-for-hire have been around for nearly as long as there's been mystery fiction. It wasn't until Dashiell Hammett came along, however, with his Sam Spade, the Continental Op and other detectives, that the private eye story was brought down to street level where it belongs, so to speak.

In degrees of depravity and perversity, here is a book tougher and rougher than any of Hammett's, by far, but of course you do have to realize that this is several generations of consciousness-raising later. Some of the scenes that occur in the course of Harry Stoner's search for a missing girl would undoubtedly make a Marquis de Sade at least momentarily queasy.

Nor is Valin the new Raymond Chandler--the first chapter in particular seems desperately overwritten--but as a journeyman wordsmith he learns quickly. Once begun it's easy to find yourself vicariously trapped in the grimier depths of Cincinnati's dingier sections, uncovering with private eye Stoner a hidden underground world of predatory sex and bloodseeking violence.

Stoner is hired by a dirty old man whose 16-year-old living companion has run away. He has pictures of her, of the kind not sold under counters, but in back rooms only. Harry fears the worst.

As a rescuer, Stoner is deliberately not cast in the Travis McGee philosophy/fantasy mold. The job is hopeless, and he knows it, yet he's idealist enough to continue hunting for those responsible for whatever's happened to Cindy Ann. His romantic liaison with a waitress named Jo is enjoyable, but it is not likely to continue with the success that Robert Parker's Spenser has found with Susan Silverman.

The key intended here instead is realism. The activities

taking place in *The Lime Pit* may not always be wholly appetizing, but they are morbidly fascinating. And while Harry Stoner may be the consumate iconoclast in many regards, he's still a superb example of the closest thing we have today to a knight in shining armor. (A minus)*

Mike Fredman. *You Can Always Blame the Rain.* St. Martins, 1980, 132 pp., $8.95. First published in the U.K. by P. Elek, 1978.

And if Harry Stoner can be considered a member of the knighthood, trying to rescue damsels in distress, so also in his way is Willie Halliday, the British private eye making his American debut. That both Fredman and Halliday are English may or may not have a great deal to do with it, but the action here is noticeably more refined than much of anything found in Valin's deliberately shocking expose of false Midwestern piety.

But, needless to say, there are similarities. There are pictures, and one of the daughters that Halliday is hired to protect is nude in them--but that is all we are told about them. There are also some references to Moroccan white slave traffic, but perhaps thankfully we are spared any further details.

Willie Halliday is a vegetarian, by the way, and he neither smokes nor drinks. He is well-versed in the history of Eastern religions, seems to have a good deal of money on his own, and none of the girls he attracts, which obviously includes his new secretary, ends up in bed with him. His first case is entertaining fun, in a quiet, genteel sort of way, but especially in comparison to a book like *The Lime Pit*, hard-boiled detective buffs are going to end up wondering just what scandal it is that he's saving the girls from. (C)*

Mark Carrel. *The Emerald.* Hale, 1971, 191 pp.

In the April 1978 issue of *The Armchair Detective*, Al Hubin, in announcing the forthcoming, long-awaited publication of his Edgar-winning *Bibliography*, also reported the staggering news (well, it was in some quarters) of a writer with even more books to his credit than the formidably prodigious John Creasey.

Mark Carrel is one of the at least 61 bylines of Lauran Bosworth Paine, who, although American and living in this country, has been published almost only in England. Through 1972, Hubin goes on to say, Paine had written 600 books, and so who knows how many by this time!

Not all of this huge output has been mystery fiction, however, and so Creasey presumably will hold onto his title of King of the Mystery Thriller for some time to come. And Paine/et al. is still completely unknown in this country. It's taken me until now to find a British dealer who had one of his books he was willing to send me. This is it.

And, to tell you the truth, it wasn't worth the wait. It pretends to be a police procedural. Homicide Inspectors Earl Talmadge and Mike Gargan hunt down the killer of His Honor Judge Delaney, found with his stomach blown out (not in) on a

Santa Monica beach. What's wrong is that the ensuing pressure
from the media and political higher-ups for them to solve the
case is seldom mentioned and certainly never felt. Talmadge
and Gargan operate as though within a bubble of reality that
completely surrounds them and follows them everywhere, pro-
tecting and isolating them from the outside world.
   Remarkably, Talmadge and Gargan seem to be equals--sharing
their thoughts in fine Pat-and-Mike fashion upon the case,
upon each other's personal habits, and upon the hamstringing
restrictions placed upon their work by lawyers. It is, in
fact, difficult to tell them apart.
   Evidence points very quickly to the killer, and the only
problem remaining is how they're going to prove it. Conti-
nuity--as regards information the D.A.'s man either gives them
or gets from them, depending on whether you're reading p.136
or p. 158--could definitely stand improving. And in the It
Never Rains But It Pours department, on p. 114 Gargan slugs a
prisoner--see my earlier comment on the Howes/Lucias affair.
   Well, in a sense it was self-defense, and in Carrel/
Paine's defense it can be said that he has an entertaining
writing style. On the evidence presented so far, it's nevertheless clear that there's little reason for us to start
mobbing the next flight to England for more of his work.
(C minus)

Dick Francis. *Whip Hand*. Harper & Row, 1979, 293 pp., $9.95.

   Thanks to some fine exposure on public television's
recent venture into mystery drama, this the latest of Dick
Francis' novels on racetrack chicanery has been flirting these
past few weeks with the lower extremities of various best-
seller lists.
   Mystery fans may not be so pleased and delighted with this
state of affairs once they realize that Harper & Row have been
pushing it as straight fiction rather than what it actually
is--a straightforward private eye detective thriller. But of
course, as everyone knows, private eye stories just don't sell.
   Sid Halley, the jockey who lost a hand in a previous
Francis adventure, has had some success recently as a private
investigator dealing largely in horsey matters. Perhaps too
much success for his own good. When the villains see him
coming, they think they know what it will take to scare him
off.
   And they're not so very far from wrong. Halley has to
come to some strong grips with himself before he can start
tackling the end of the case. But in spite of all the soul-
searching, or more likely because of it, the pace seems to
plod more than it has in much of Francis' previous works. The
violence seems to be too calculated and perfunctory, and in
spite of the odds, Sid Halley comes up smelling of roses, just
as expected. (B)*

Ellis Peters. *A Morbid Taste for Bones*. Popular Library,
   1980, 256 pp., $1.95.

   Well, yes, I guess you caught me. I've always claimed not
to care for period detective fiction, be it Victorian, 12th

century, pre-Elizabethan, or what. But I liked Brother Cadfael as a character in *One Corpse Too Many*, reviewed here not so far back, so much so that when I saw this earlier book had just come out in paperback, I picked it up and started reading it while I was still in the store, and I ended up not putting it down when I got home.

Some of Cadfael's earlier, nonecclesiastical career is revealed--he was a sailor and a Crusader, very much an adventurer and a man of the world. With all this, he has found it easire to adjust to life in the monastic enclave of Shrewsbury Abbey than have some of the younger men.

In fact, rather than arising from a civil disturbance of the sort that produced the murder mystery of *One Corpse Too Many*, the crisis this time focuses inwardly, upon the personalities and the not always totally spiritual ambitions of various of the brothers. In particular, it is Prior Robert's dream of removing the bones of Saint Winifred to England from her burial place in her home country of Wales that initiates the sequence of events that culminates, not unexpectedly, in murder.

Thwarted romance is also involved. In Cadfael's objective eye toward such matters, God often needs a little helping hand from man. The culprit is easily spotted, thanks to better-than-average characterization--could this by why some people object so loudly to characterization in detective stories? Are mysteries and good writing incompatible? I refuse to think so.

Occasionally the dialogue does wax exceedingly biblical in tone, and some tolerance for it has to be developed. And perhaps it shouldn't have, but a reference to a *steel*-tipped arrow surprised me a little. (B)

Barbara Betcherman. *Suspicions*. Putnam's, 1980, 410 pp., $10.95.

While neither of the following two books falls greatly into the category conventions of the "romantic suspense" novel, or whatever it is that they're calling Gothics these days, both of them feature a heroine in trouble. And while both of the leading ladies are married, each of them is forced by circumstances to find an independent identity for herself.

On the face of it, Sylvia West in this book would seem to have an easire time of it. She is a successful criminal lawyer in her own right, plus she has a home in the suburbs, two fine young boys and an equally successful husband. That their marriage is in trouble, which it is, is due in large part to John West's old-world views on women, and their subservient place in the order of things.

It still comes as a complete surprise to Sylvia when he disappears one day completely. He doesn't show up for work, he leaves behind no message of any kind. The police, while outwardly sympathetic, are of no help at all, even when a body claimed to be that of John West is recovered from a fiery automobile accident in Florida, in the questionable company of a Times Square hooker.

Sylvia West finds herself alone, at odds against the rest of the world, which has heard her story before. She finds herself slowly uncovering a conspiracy against her, one of

international dimensions, with her husband's disappearing act only a minor facet of its world-wide activities.
If men can get themselves into such trouble, à la Robert Ludlum, the book seems to ask, why then can't women.
But the book is too long. As readers totally accustomed to vicarious paranoia, we know there's a plot of lies working against Sylvia West long before she is finally convinced of it. We've read the story before. If there were any suspense it disappears quickly in a flowing stream of overabundant wordiness. (C)*

Dorothy Salisbury Davis. *Scarlet Night*. Scribner's, 1980, 244 pp., $9.95.

Even before Sylvia West in *Suspicions* finds her husband gone, she already has a strong sense of independence. By way of contrast, Julie Hayes in this book finds herself with an extremely happy marriage and yet too much time on her hands. Her husband Jeff is a newspaper reporter, and he is often on the road.
In his absence, Julie tries writing a novel, thinks about becoming a gossip columnist, and gets mixed up in the world of art collectors, the honest and the not-so-honest.
Scarlet Night is also the name of a painting, and not really a very good one. So why then the furious demand for it when the artist very nearly makes Julie a present of it?
This is a caper novel. Thanks to a Nero Wolfian porno king named Sweets Romano, it neatly turns into a counter-caper story as well. It's not very believable, it must be admitted, but there is a lot more fun involved here than anything at all that develops in the strictly sober-sided *Suspicions*.
In that book it is Sylvia West's chic urbanity that helps her most in seeing her through her crisis. Acting nervously against her own inherently retiring nature, in *Scarlet Night* Julie Hayes left me the distinct impression of being the braver of the two. (B)*

Michael Z. Lewin. *Night Cover*. Berkley, 1980, 262 pp., $1.95.

False advertising!
This was supposed to be an Albert Sampson mystery, or at least that's what is said on the front cover. As you may have heard, Albert Samson is a private eye, and his reputation is that he is the cheapest in Indianapolis. I read and reported on another of his adventures a while ago, and while it doesn't seem to me that I recall him giving out green stamps, I do remember enjoying it.
Samson appears in all of perhaps seven pages of this one.
In center court instead is Lt. Roy Powder, the cop in charge of the Indianapolis Night Shift for nearly nineteen years. His dominating, gruff personality has grown now until it overshadows most of his cases, two of which involve a school's missing cashbox, a Maoist hippie, and a runaway girl.
It's not surprising that when they meet, which they do, Powder and the outspoken Samson do not get along very well.
But Powder also uncovers a series of multi-murder crimes and undergoes a change-of-life that surprises even him. In

other words, in case you haven't realized it yet, this is not a private eye story at all. It's a book with a gritty feel of real small-city police work, enhanced greatly by the deductive instincts of a veteran cop, who has sharpened and tempered them by years of experience on the job.

It's a book I'm glad I read, but it sure wasn't what I expected when I picked it off the shelf. (B-)

Patrick Quentin. *Puzzle for Fiends*. Avon, 1979, 222 pp., $2.25.

Since late last year Avon has quietly been reissuing the Quintin "Puzzle" series, although unfortunately they have not been bothered to publish them in chronological order. This was the first one they did, and it's one of the later ones in the series. But I hope you've seen them--the attempts at period photography on the covers came out well, and they're certainly designed for eye-appeal--and even though the price seems a little stiff, if you've never read any of them, here's a part of what the Golden Age of Mysteries was all about.

As a detective, Peter Duluth was purely an amateur. As a civilian, he was usually a theatrical producer; his wife Iris, a glamorous Hollywood star. In this book she makes only the briefest of appearances, however, as she's off on an extended overseas entertainment tour just as Peter arrives home, Navy discharge in hand.

And for that matter, neither does Peter do any producing, since in true *tour de force* fashion he wakes up from a mugging attack to find himself without a memory to call his own, casts on both arm and leg, and being taken for someone called Gordy Friend, and by the latter's own family, no less. Still, there's nothing like waking up from a nap and finding yourself rich, is there?

Nevertheless, accident and all, Peter has not been weakened enough mentally to sense that appearances, as always, can be deceiving. He soon learns that he is a central figure in a small fiendish scenario involving both himself and a will about to be contested in unusual fashion by the West Coast branch of the Aurora (Minn.) Clean Living League.

A number of nicely thought out twists follow before Duluth finds his befogged way out of this mess, with one of them depending greatly on--how does the riddle go?--a "particularly nasty spell of weather." Well done--Bravo! in fact-- with a couple of scenes decidedly more excitingly erotic than anything you could ever find in the complete works of, say, Christie, Carr and Gardner, combined. (A)

H.R.F. Keating. *The Murder of the Maharajah*. Doubleday, 1980, 259 pp., $10.00.

If there were an award designed to be given every year to some new mystery in the memory of the late Agatha Christie-- there isn't, and why not?--this is the book that would make Keating this year's hands-down winner. Not only does it owe a great deal to Mrs. Christie in time, the year 1930, and in exotic locale, India, when that land was still a formidable bulwark of the British Empire, but in atmosphere, characters (some of whom are actually seen reading a Christie novel) and leisurely pace as well.

The maharajah, never one to be crossed, is also inordinately fond of April Fool's jokes, but one--a limousine's plugged exhaust pipe--quickly comes home to roost (backfires?) when a plugged shotgun barrel is discovered to be the immediate cause of His Highness' demise.

There are only a limited number of suspects, which should sound familiar, but even so D.S.P. Howard's investigation into the case makes little initial headway, not even with the most highly enthusiastic help of the palace's schoolmaster. Not until, that is, in grandly extravagant and artificial fashion-- and comes the reminder that very seldom are mysteries written like this taking place in today's penny-pinching economies-- an enormous royal banquet is recreated in the smallest detail, staged solely to help a murderer reveal himself.

Lots of red herrings, you can bet on that, a thwarted romance or two, and a clue I'm willing to wager a bevy of Imperial sandgrouse that you'll never spot, no matter how earnestly and devoutly you try.

And for those who have followed Keating's long career in writing detective mysteries up to now, there is a last line that is utterly untoppable. (A minus)*

Miles Burton. *The Man with the Tattooed Face.* Doubleday/Crime Club, 1937, 278 pp.

Immediately preceding page one you'll find a map of the "downtown" section of the village of Faston Bishop, including all the salient details that describe the locale where the dead man is found, and believe me, it--the map, that is--gets a full workout.

The victim is the man with the tattoos on his face. While he earned his living as a common laborer on several of the farms surrounding Faston Bishop, he also seems to be working very much below his true station in life. Rumors are also that he was not averse to carrying on an affair or two with some of the wives in the vicinity.

The detective is Inspector Arnold of the C.I.D., and within the first 100 pages he has a theory that fits all the facts. Obviously it doesn't, however, and on page 173 is a timetable that soon leads to the discovery of the fatal flaw in his hypothesis.

Arnold's friend Desmond Merrion insists that the solution to the crime must come directly from the dead man's unknown past. Arnold's stubborn obstinacy to this plan of thought is quite inexplicable.

Other than these two divergent approaches to the investigation of the murder, the two amicable crime-solvers leave little to distinguish themselves, one from the other--or from countless other featureless detectives from the "Golden Age". But the seductive lure and the leisurely pace of the classical mystery novel, told in simplest terms here as a puzzle in pure detection, these are what you'll find in abundance, on every page. (B)

George Bagby. *Country and Fatal.* Doubleday/Crime Club, 1980,

181 pp., $8.95.

Need further proof that riding the Manhattan subway system can be dangerous to your health? On page one of Bagby's latest mystery-adventure, you'll find him being pushed off the Times Square station platform smack into the path of an oncoming train.

A series of such attacks has surprisingly nothing to do with Bagby's friendship with Inspector Schmidt of Homicide, and the many cases they've worked on together. Rather it has everything to do with an ex-con country singer named Shad McGee (almost married to the phenomenally shelf-bosomed Lucinda Belle), who wants Bagby to give him a hand with his memoirs.

Names and any resemblances etc. etc. entirely coincidental. Not your usual background for a detective murder mystery, but it's fun, and what's more, the clues are fair. In fact, there's one in particular that should be obvious. I really don't know what I was thinking of. (B minus)

Helen McCloy. *Burn This*. Dodd, Mead, 1980, 182 pp., $7.95.

Here's a book that brings back memories of murder mysteries past. Until this one, Miss McCloy's most recent novels have had, sad to say, little of anything to recommend them. Their focus has been on current topics like terrorist kidnappings and at least the fringes of international espionage, but when an author just doesn't seem to feel comfortable with a story, the reader's interest will wander as well.

But back in the 1940's and early 1950's Helen McCloy did write several still very well regarded mysteries, many of them starring her criminologist-psychologist detective Dr. Basil Willing. This being the first appearance of the good doctor in twelve or so years, mystery fans have been looking forward to it with some anticipation.

The premise is fine--an apartment building full of writers learns that one of them has uncovered the secret identity of a well-hated book critic (a most unreasonable reason for murder, however, if ever I heard one)--but the promise is not fulfilled.

Dr. Willing does not make an appearance until page 99, and too much has happened for us to see him filled in properly. The pace is fast, and in the haste a clue the reader might use in advance to help substantiate a motive for murder seems to have been neglected.

The early goings on are highly overdramatized as well, with a good deal of shouting and posing going on. And so, whth the shaky bit of deduction that goes on at the end, the book reads like a phonograph record would sound of the hole in the middle were but a fraction of an inch off center. The book needs filling out; instead it's been pared to the quick.

Not a very good omen, you might say, for a successful return to the "classical" detective story. If it weren't for the Keating book, reviewed here just a while back, I'd have to agree with you. (C)*

Alisa Craig. *A Pint of Murder*. Doubleday/Crime Club, 1980, 184 pp., $8.95.

Of all the detective murder mysteries that have ever been committed in fiction, only a surprisingly small number of them have been tackled by a member of the Royal Canadian Mounted Police. Tackled and solved, of course. The Mounties always get their men, as everyone well knows.

Ms. Craig does what she can to remedy the situation. The case is that of the food-poisoning death of a crotchety but scrupulously careful old lady in the New Brunswick town of Pitcherville. Inspector Madoc Rhys (a Welshman!) is the Mountie who is called in to investigate. The story, well, it could be likened to a breath of fresh clear Canadian air, containing only the slightest bit of pollution, and that of the sort produced by the gossipy thoughts and attitudes of small village minds with nothing to contain them.

This is also a book for those who do not mind a little romance mixing it up with their mystery fiction. By book's end it quite definitely is clear that the Mounties almost always get their women as well. (C plus)

VERDICTS
(More Reviews)

John Rhode. *Hendon's First Case.* Collins, 1935.

   Over a period of approximately thirty-five years, John Rhode wrote seventy-two mystery novels featuring the scientist and criminologist, Dr. Priestley, and Superintendent Hanslet of Scotland Yard. In the earlier novels, especially the ones preceding *Hendon's First Case*, a more-or-less set formula was followed. Hanslet, working on a case, tells Dr. Priestley about the case, and Dr. Priestley joins in the investigation. He is quite physically active in the early novels, leaving his home to visit the scene of the murder or to talk with persons involved in the case. Dr. Priestley has a strong aversion toward making conjectures without proof, and often he delays for several chapters exposing the murderer to Hanslet while he seeks to verify every last detail. Some of the early novels are marred by his carrying this to the extreme, and by the seemingly endless discussions between Dr. Priestley and Hanslet and others.
   In *Hendon's First Case*, Rhode begins to change his formula He introduces a new continuing character, Jimmy Waghorn, who, in subsequent novels, will become more and more the principal character. Hanslet and Dr. Priestley will play smaller and smaller roles, with Dr. Priestley tending to stay at home, and Waghorn will do most of the outside work, as he does in this novel. Rhode takes advantage of a recent development in police circles, the founding of the Police College, to introduce his new character.
   When the metropolitan police force was established in london in 1829, it was a matter of policy that there should be no caste system in the police force as there was in the armed forces. In the beginning the higher ranks of the police were filled with ex-warrant and non-commissioned officers, and it was a principle of the founder, Sir Robert Peel, that vacancies in the higher ranks were to be filled by promotion from below. This principle was kept intact for more than 100 years though there were times when it resulted in an apparent lack of effective leadership.
   In 1931, Lord Trenchard was appointed Commissioner of Police. He had been one of the founders of the Royal Air Force, a military man, and his answer to the problem of shortcomings in leadership was to create a special group of potential leaders. This "officer material' was to be chosen partly from the ranks of the police and partly from outside. For their training the Hendon Metropolitan Police College was established in 1934. The first class consisted of thirty-two men, twenty chosen from within the police force and twelve from without. They were given the newly created rank of junior station inspector and put through a fifteen month course.
   One of the men in the first class was Junior Station Inspector Jimmy Waghorn. He was one of those chosen from outside the police force, after having to leave Cambridge following the death of his father. As the story opens, he has completed the course at the Police College and has had a year of

experience in various police jobs, and he has just arrived at Scotland Yard to work as a detective under the watchful eye of Superintendent Hanslet. In the first chapter Waghorn's background and training are discussed, and then Waghorn is sent out on his first case. Thus, the title of the novel.

It is a strange case, in which the most important question is how the victim, Threlfall, was murdered. Threlfall, a chemist, receives a letter from his estranged wife threatening him with something extremely unpleasant if he does not yield to her demand for a divorce. Within two days the laboratory in which Threlfall and his partner carry on their research is broken into, a bomb is planted (and explodes) in Threlfall's study, and Threlfall dies of ptomaine poisoning after dining with his partner at a restaurant. Waghorn enters the case when he is sent by Hanslet to investigate the breakin. He becomes convinced that it cannot be a coincidence that all these things have happened to Threlfall in such a short time, and he concludes that Threlfall has been murdered. But how? Ptomaines are found in the remains of a dish shared by Threlfall and his partner (who was also taken ill, but recovered), and Hanslet and Waghorn agree that no employee of the restaurant could be involved in a plot to murder threlfall. Hanslet believes that Threlfall's death is a coincidence, but since the breakin and the bombing must be solved, he allows Waghorn to stay on the case.

Waghorn finds a tangled web, involving Threlfall's wife and her love, a stranger who accosted Threlfall as he and his partner were on their way to the fatal meal, the partner himself and Threlfall's lawyer, and a coded message left by Threlfall with his lawyer. Waghorn solves the bombing and, apparently, the breakin, but he ca-not break the code of the message and he cannot explain how Threlfall was poisoned.

Meanwhile, Hanslet visits Dr. Priestley and tells him about Waghorn's case. At Dr. Priestley's request, he brings Waghorn to meet the great man. Dr. Priestley is impressed with the young man's attitude and intelligence, and he gives him his usual caution about making unsupported conjectures. Waghorn shows Dr. Priestley the coded message, and at a glance the latter breaks the code. Waghorn decodes the message, and its contents suggest to him the identity of the murderer. He moves to confront the suspect, and ends up in the hospital, himself a victim of ptomaine poisoning. Dr. Priestley takes up the investigation, and after a visit to the lawyer's office, where he learns the contents of the coded message, he describes exactly how Threlfall was poisoned. With that, the case solves itself.

In one of the chapters, Hanslet and Dr. Priestley talk about the Police College and the philosophy behind its founding. Hanslet's view is that of a policeman who has advanced through the ranks in the traditional way. He is willing to go along with the College--as an experiment--but he fears that it will cause some morale problems in the ranks. In this he is correct, for the members of the police force, represented by the Police Federation, were not so tolerant of the Police College as Hanslet. There were cries of militarism and caste system (exactly what Peel had hoped to avoid) from the Federation and its friends in Parliament, and there were bitter complaints about the selecting of men for the College from outside the force. But the conflict between the Police Federation and the police authority was not allowed to proceed to its natural conclusion. With the start of the war the Police College was closed, and after the war a new training institution was organized along different lines. Those who are interested can read more about the history of the police in England, and about the Police College in particular, in the excellent book, *A History of Police in England and Wales*, by T. A. Critchley (Constable, 1967; revised edition, 1978).

Arthur Rollo, a character in some of the later novels of Freeman Wills Crofts, is another fictional product of the Hendon Police College. Are there others? (Paul McCarthy)

Loren D. Estleman. *Motor City Blues*. Houghton Mifflin, 1980, $9.95.

The raw, unionized world of Detroit, overshadowed by the auto industry, provides a suitably grimy environment for a principled private eye to roam, correcting the wrongs of the world. Amos Walker's job of finding a mobster's ward who has run off to engage in pornographic films seems uncomplicated at first. But before it is all resolved Army Intelligence and a black reform candidate are prominently in the act. Walker goes through a few beatings that would keep normal men in the hospital for a week. Walker provides swift adventure as he fits the pieces of a complex scheme together. Unfortunately, Estleman tries too hard in his writing, impeding the reader with strained descriptions and excess detail about Detroit. Hard-boiled fans will probably enjoy it, others will not be as impressed. (Fred Dueren)

Felice Picano. *The Lure*. Delacourt Press, 1979.

When Professor Noel Cummings heard the scream of a man being killed he was drawn into a world he'd hardly known existed. Being an innocent, he agreed to help the police trap a vicious killer who was preying on New York's gay population. The best way to trap the killer was for Noel to enter the gay world and let the killer locate him. But Noel also entered a world similar to that experienced by spies--little is what it seems and he's never sure who is a friend or for how long. As Picano develops the people and atmosphere, the criminal elements of the book often get left behind. His attention to Noel's involvement with Buddy Vega (cop or traitor?), Randy Navore (friend or victim?), and Eric Redfern (a killer or mastermind of a new society?), and Noel's reactions to his feelings and involvements are the main focus of the novel. There are a few flaws in the plotting that point question marks at some characters, but on the whole it is a powerful book with an unusual, but not unique, murder motive and method. (Fred Dueren)

Angus Ross. *The Hamburg Switch*. Walker, 1980, $9.95.

Agent Mark Farrow's latest task is to get defecting scientist Eberhart Jagersberg out of East Germany. Young Mackenzie, on his first assignment, provides elegant competence and contrast to Farrow's nervous grouchiness as the complications and problems of the case grow. Unknown assailants waylay Farrow, several freelance agents get involved, and finally, after Farrow crosses into East Germany to get him, Jagersberg is whisked from Farrow's arms. Determined to recover Jagersberg for England, Farrow plays his own game, wrapping up the thriller in a rather subdued rescue scene. (Fred Dueren)

Margaret Truman. *Murder in the White House*. Arbor House, 1980, 235 pp., $9.95.

Both Harry and Bess Truman were long known as devotees of mystery fiction, and this delightful addiction seems to have been passed on to their daughter Margaret, who has now presented herself as a detective novelist. Whatever else can be said about her first effort in this field, its central elements are certainly appropriate to her background, with the presidential living quarters as the murder scene and the members and closest associates of the fictional First Family as prime suspects. Secretary of State Lansard Blaine, a brilliant and egotistical ex-professor of diplomatic history, is garroted to death with a piece of thin wire in the Lincoln Sitting Room on the second floor of the White House. Ron Fairbanks, a young Washington lawyer serving as Special Counsel to President Robert Lang Webster, is appointed by his chief to head the ensuing investigation, which stretches over most of the book and reveals the dead man to have been an insatiable womanizer, a taker of financial and sexual bribes, a blackmailer--in short, one whose death might have been devoutly wished by countless persons, perhaps even by the President himself.

Murder in the White House is not a study of character or scene, for the sleuths and suspects are uniformly dull and the official background routinely sketched in. It's not a police procedural, for the police are never seen doing a blessed thing to solve this murder. It's not a suspense novel, for of suspense there is next to none. It's not an exercise in style, for the book is cluttered with awkward parentheses, sentences ending in dots, eccentric compound words like beachhouse and tenniscourt, and fractured disjunctives like niether ... or. It's not a fair-play detective story, for there are no clues, the murderer simply confesses at the climax, at least one loose end of the elementary plot is left untidily dangling, and as for the puzzle which may have tantalized some readers--how did the killer make the bloody loop of wire vanish from a White House ringed with investigators?--the appropriate character cavalierly tells us that "I disposed of it." End of subject.

Margaret Truman's first novel is something of a soap opera, especially during the climactic midnight confrontation in the Oval Office, and something of a love song to a fictional President, who unsurprisingly turns out to be a tower of noble integrity in crisis, despite his policies and outward appearances. The many things wrong with the book, however, suggest strongly that she did write it herself, or at worst that whatever ghost she had didn't help much. It's an amiable, unchallengeing, easy-to-read story whose structure and content seem made to order for a TV movie, even to the abundant cameo scenes for aging special guest stars. It is being heavily promoted and will make a great deal of money. (Francis M. Nevins, Jr.)

Alice Laurance and Isaac Asimov, eds. *Who Done It?* Houghton Mifflin, 1980, 229 pp., $9.95.

    In his 1938 anthology of short mysteries *Challenge to the Reader*, editor Ellery Queen assembled twenty-five detective stories, altered the name of the sleuth who solved each case, and invited readers to use the clues in the mater and manner of each tale to name both its detective and its author. The only trouble with the book was that its concept eliminated all possible audiences: readers who weren't versed in mystery fiction at all found the identification game impossible to play, while those who had dipped even a little into the genre saw the challenge as absurdly simple, especially since Queen had left unchanged the names of well-known supporting characters in each adventure. More than forty years later, editors Laurance and Asimov are again challenging readers to identify authors, but they've improved on Queen's concept by printing only non-series stories that have never been published before. The result is that neither familiarity with a tale through a prior magazine appearance nor familiarity with a recurring series character can help the reader. If he or she is to spot the author it can only be through cracking the cipher in which the writers' names are given or through recognizing the amalgam of style and subject which makes each good writer unique.
    Of the seventeen authors whose work is gathered here, the reasonably well-read mystery fan should be able to identify at least a few: Robert Bloch from his sense of ghoulish fun, Edward D. Hoch from his love of codes and locked-room puzzles and Ellery Queen-like fair-play deductions, John D. MacDonald and Janwillem van de Wetering from the indefinable sensibility that seems to permeate every word they write. But even the most devoted reader of Bill Pronzini will be unlikely to guess which tale is his, and a few of the contributors who shall be nameless are just not well enough known to be identifiable stylistically. The stories themselves range from excellent (MacDonald's and van de Wetering's) to average, and Asimov's introductory essay on style is amusing without being terribly profound. *Who Done It?* is something like those gift boxes of assorted cheeses one receives at Christmastime, a neatly wrapped package of seventeen petite portions, satisfying to the palate even if we can't tell the Edam from the Gouda. (Francis M. Nevins, Jr.)

THE DOCUMENTS IN THE CASE
(Letters)

From Jim Goodrich, 5 Ulster Road, New Paltz, NY 12561:
Just received *Mystery* #3 and agree, as usual, with Marv Lachman's assessment of it. The mag is most definitely "designed to turn a profit" which is a noble goal as long as we buffs do not continue to be ignored. To Sandy Sandulo: Tartan Books Sales offers the books that are returned from libraries that rent McNaughton titles--both are owned by Bro Dart, a major library supplies manufacturer. To John Harwood: being part of the over-50 crowd I remember "Quick as a Flash" and "Lights out." According to Dunning's *Tune in Yesterday*, "Quick" ran on Sunday afternoons, so probably preceded "The Shadow." The "Lights Out" show I vividly remember was the famous "Chicken Heart" that consumed the world. Yummy.
[*More, from a later letter:*]
My Lord, you do ramble (mile-wise, not verbally--except in the case of Rex Stout). Back home again in Arkansas doesn't roll off the tongue as well as in Indiana. May you stay stationary for a couple of volumes of TMF. Re volume 4, number 2, I thank Jeff Banks for his comments on the delightfully immodest Miss Blaise. I also must again publically contribute to the praise so rightfully bestowed on the modest Steve Lewis's reviews--they are superb, as are those of the pubber, Steve Mertz, and Mike Nevins. As for Dave Doerrer and Black John Smith, most of the Halfaday Creek books I've seen were Triangle reprints. I'll join Dave in labeling the tales as mysteries. Don't believe most of us will find Hendryx in the catalog of our local friendly library, however, or in a college library like mine. Since Ilse Goldsmith has written a couple of books, she is eminently qualified to do an article on Amanda Cross as you requested, Guy.
Have found no evidence that *Twentieth Century Crime and Mystery Writers* has been published, so that may explain why you have not received a copy. [*My copy of TCCMW has since arrived, and I have spent many pleasurable hours with it already. I recommend it highly, even to non contributors who will have to pay the full price for the monster volume. No doubt we will have at least one in-depth review in the next issue of TMF (hint, hint).*] Between Kelley and Lewis I don't know if I should *Look for Rachel Wallace* or not! Bill Crider: Pan has issued all of the Modesty titles, with the possible exception of the latest, in paperback.

From Jim O'Donnell, 77, Hazelville Rd., Birmingham, B28 9QD, England:
Many thanks for TMF 4:2--very enjoyable.
The actor that starred in the Quiller TV series was Michael Jayston. Incidentally, I don't believe that my handwriting can be better than your's, or any one else's for that matter. [*Believe it, Jim.*]
There is a further Modesty Blaise book, *Dragon's Claw*, published in hardback by Souvenir Press in 1978 and paperback by Pan in 1979....
P.S. What is "The Not So Private Eye"? [*It's another fanzine--see "The Line-Up" in the next TMF for details.*]

From Fred Dueren, 2409 Oakwood Blvd., Wausau, WI 54401:

I'm sorry about the misinformation about the books in Dell's new series of mysteries to come out. I was relying on an article in *Publisher's Weekly*. Since then I've also learned that Robert Barnard's *Death of a Mystery Writer* has also been published in the U.S. already. By Scribners, I believe. I've also picked up one of the Raven House Mysteries, *Murder Takes a Wife* by James A. Howard. It is a reprint from 1958. It lists other books in the series as:

Mary Challis, *Crimes Past*
Mary Ann Taylor, *Red Is for Shrouds*
Robert B. Gillespie, *The Crossword Mystery*
Anne Burton, *The Dear Departed*
John Wolfe, *Drilling for Death*
Richard A. Moore, *Death in the Past*
Dell Shannon, *Rain with Violence*.

www.ingramcontent.com/pod-product-compliance
Lightning Source LLC
Chambersburg PA
CBHW031434040426
42444CB00006B/811